5

You Really
Need to Know
John Jervis

greenfinch

Contents

Introduction

Everything, as American graphic designer Paul Rand once said, is design. A flamboyant claim when made in the 1990s, it's pretty much a given today. Signing a global treaty or developing a space programme, making a shopping list or booking a holiday – almost any premeditated action can now be considered an act of design.

In that context, this is a necessarily conservative book, taking a Western-oriented walk through the emergence of industrial design. Even within that limited compass, however, there is an astonishing richness, some of which, hopefully, is captured in these 50 ideas. They are tackled in a loosely chronological order, from early predecessors and progenitors, to the arrival and glory days of Modernism, to the more fractured present.

Over that period, design – originally derived from the Italian for 'drawing' – has become one of the most powerful words in language, seen as offering vital solutions to the world's challenges, embodying an abiding commitment to improving lives, and comprising a fundamental part of what makes us human. All this, while carrying a towering luxury industry in its wake. So it's probably worth retaining just a little scepticism about the use of the term. Sometimes 'thinking' may well be a more accurate one – or the better approach to a problem.

Inevitably, this book draws on a wide range of specialist resources that I don't have space to mention. The least I can do is to suggest that, if you find one or other idea particularly intriguing, do go out and read more about it. You'll find authors who are immeasurably better informed and equipped to do these subjects real justice. I've hugely enjoyed reading their work in recent months, and perhaps you might too.

John Jervis

01 Mass Production

As a term, 'mass production' is confusing. How else would you describe the billions of coins made during the Roman Empire (27 BCE–476 CE), or the huge quantities of ceramics produced for export and home markets in China during the Song dynasty (960–1279 CE)? But today, it usually suggests something more specific: a production process incorporating manufacturing methods that evolved during the Industrial Revolution and were fully realized during the early 20th century. These include automated machinery, standardized interchangeable components, moving assembly lines and the division of labour, in which individuals were allocated specific roles in the production process, employing specialized skills related to that role.

Military beginnings

There are many competing claims around the origins of mass production – difference in emphasis plays a role, as does nationalism – but the American version encompasses many of its components. In 1798, Eli Whitney received an order from the US government to produce 10,000 muskets at his Connecticut armoury, with standardized parts that could be swapped in and out, facilitating repair and, in theory, manufacture, but requiring high levels of accuracy. Water-driven machinery was introduced, lessening the need for skilled labour and increasing specialization in workers' tasks. Whitney's levels of success and innovation are highly debatable. French arms manufacturers had already experimented with interchangeability, while efforts to optimize screw threads were underway in Germany. In Britain, hundreds of thousands of standardized rigging blocks were manufactured in Portsmouth's Royal Dockyards from 1803 using all-metal machinery created by French-born engineer Marc Isambard Brunel. But Whitney's work gave additional impetus to the spread of assembly lines and the development of precision machinery to produce standard components and test their consistency.

Better futures

Gradually, interchangeability and mechanization were applied to less dangerous ends in the United States, including sewing machines and bicycles, and becoming known, collectively, as the American System.

With the implementation of 'scientific management' in the country's factories from the 1890s – time-and-motion studies to determine the most efficient layouts – the era of mass production had arrived, promoting the quality, availability and affordability of consumer goods for mass audiences, improving the lives of many. Perhaps the definitive example is Henry Ford's introduction of moving assembly lines to his Michigan plant in 1913, implementing the ideas of Frederick Winslow Taylor, the 'founding father' of scientific management. As well as economies of scale and time, these innovations led to another familiar consequence of mass production. Unhappiness with the relentless and repetitive nature of the new working conditions had to be alleviated by doubling the salaries of plant employees.

> **Mass production is not merely quantity production, for this may be had with none of the requisites of mass production. Nor is it merely machine production, which also may exist without any resemblance to mass production. Mass production is the focusing upon a manufacturing project of the principles of power, accuracy, economy, system, continuity, and speed.**
> Henry Ford, 1926

Designing mass production

Despite the impression given by such origin stories, mass production is not a static process, but one constantly being redesigned in response to changes in technology, regulations, raw materials, supply chains and global politics. Scientific management still plays a role – it is now possible to implement a constant feedback loop gathering data on a massive scale – but experimentation, innovation and improvisation are also vital. Obvious examples are the harnessing of new technologies, from the groundbreaking addition of robotic arms to assembly lines by General Motors in 1961, to the gradual adoption of 3D-printing in recent years, providing short runs of components and machine parts quickly and conveniently, but at a high cost per unit.

Such changes are often seen as having negative impacts on working culture, but they can also be positive. In the 1950s, pioneering efforts were made to introduce 'just-in-time' manufacturing – holding raw materials only for immediate needs, and producing goods when

Innovation

Mass production has a difficult relationship with innovation. To remain competitive, processes and products must constantly be refined, and the speed and quantities involved should allow for constant iteration and improvement. Yet, by its nature, mass production relies on complex global supply chains, with multiple firms providing parts that must operate to consistent international standards to remain interchangeable across products, companies and countries. To alter one component in a single item can have a significant impact across a business, increasing costs, timelines and prices. Similarly, assembly lines are expensive to build, as are distribution networks – stopping production to accommodate change is a costly undertaking. Improvements in 3D-printing are gradually alleviating some of these issues, but they still play a major role in allowing smaller companies with lower budgets, less infrastructure and shorter production runs to play a disproportionate role in design innovation.

required, not in advance – to reduce waste and increase the competitiveness of Toyota's plants. This led to the establishment of teams of employees, each encouraged to contribute collectively to the continuous improvement of processes. To pursue increased productivity via a culture of collaboration and communication was an implied rebuke to scientific management's dehumanizing approach to efficiency. In the 1990s, this mindset had evolved into an all-encompassing 'lean production' methodology, prioritizing the creation of teams to harness employees' insights and talents, and fostering a culture that encourages feedback and reduces power dynamics. Such concerns might more naturally be associated with the creative sector, so it is not so surprising that lean principles have been adopted by such companies as Pixar and Spotify.

Where next?

Customization has long been hailed as the next big challenge to norms in mass production. Improvements in 3D-printing technology, computer-aided design and artificial intelligence are key to realizing this scenario, facilitating the rapid manufacture of both prototypes and purpose-built components, while allowing designs to be optimized on an iterative basis, and predicting future preferences and demands. Mass production will need to evolve in turn, for instance by the increased adoption of cellular manufacturing, in which small 'cells' of employees and machinery are grouped together, each dedicated to the production of specific products or components, but with the skills and resources to shift quickly to processing similar products, enhancing flexibility and efficiency.

A more significant challenge to current models of mass production might come with the acceptance by international bodies of the concept of degrowth, ending the current prioritization given to ever-increasing economic productivity. By shifting to alternative metrics around sustainable development, strong public services and increased well-being, both ecological and social breakdown could perhaps be avoided. If adopted, mass production's principles and practices would require profound rethinks, as would those of the design industry.

The condensed idea
Automation for affordability, availability and prosperity

02 Design Reform

On a semi-regular basis, countries have a crisis of confidence about design. One took place in Great Britain in the mid-19th century – a meltdown so extreme that it gave birth to the world's first design museum, sited in its own extensive cultural quarter; the first-ever 'world's fair', attended by more than six million people; and an extraordinary 'palace of crystal' in London's Hyde Park.

Towards a common standard

In part, this situation emerged from international trade's growing importance to the British economy. Reliant on exports of manufactured goods to bring in the food needed for its growing population, and the raw materials needed to sustain its ageing factories, Britain was confronted by markets growing their own industries, and erecting trade barriers to protect them. It was clear that British manufacturers needed to improve the quality of their output to flourish. Confronted by the superior artistry on display at a series of national exhibitions in Paris – a symptom of France's own anguish at its laggardly industrialization – many in Britain saw design as key to improving industrial production, international exports and national prestige.

Yet this self-doubt had other causes too. In a country growing richer, the conspicuous inequality, squalor and ongoing social unrest all suggested a society in need of fundamental reform – political, economic, moral and religious. Again, design was seen as having a fundamental role to play in improving standards in industry and education, and increasing wealth and cohesion across the classes.

To the modern mind, it can be hard to grasp the equivalence in which Victorians held the design of society and the design of manufactures. Yet a common standard of taste, expressing national character and moral truths, could bind the country together, building a commitment to utility over vanity, and a shared vision of the country's essential qualities. That this standard should be determined by a cultural elite, and imposed on those beneath, was taken as a given. A number of polemicists emerged – design reformers – arguing vigorously about the precise nature of this single absolute standard, and how to achieve it, but they did so in the belief that that they were promoting social and moral welfare, improving the conditions and education of the masses.

The message of good design

Some of this fervour centred on deploring the excessive and eclectic ornamentation applied to industrial goods, which failed to match their true purpose, and also the slapdash copying of historic forms. Both these were seen as resulting from manufacturers prioritizing economy and pandering to new, volatile consumer markets willing to follow their own paths and preferences. Re-exerting control of taste related to fundamental concerns about a fracturing society – thus the urgency of spreading the message of good design through exhibitions, museums and manuals of household hints. It was clear that a new breed of artists was needed – ones who could act as intermediaries between manufacturers and markets, creating goods suitable for mass-production, attractive to consumers, and embodying approved design principles. Dedicated design schools were needed.

To all these ends, a committee was set up in 1835 by the UK parliament 'to inquire into the best means of extending a knowledge of the Arts and the Principle of Design among the People (especially the Manufacturing Population) of the Country'. Two years later, the first Government School of Design was founded, after much debate on whether the curriculum should focus on practical experience or fine arts when equipping students with the skills to create designs for industrially produced goods – a diverse mix of pattern-making, anatomical drawing and botanical studies resulted.

One of the loudest voices was that of Henry Cole, later to deliver the Great Exhibition, direct the Victoria and Albert Museum, and found *The Journal of Design* to promote 'the germs of a style that England of the 19th century may call its own'. For Cole, an alliance between industry and design was key to ensuring the quality (and export) of British goods, while it was incumbent on those with culture to educate the masses: 'Taste has its principles as well as morals, which people understand and know. . .I think to act upon the principle "everyone to his taste" would be as mischievous as "everyone to his morals".'

With similar views on the role of design, architect Augustus Pugin is most famous for his powerful interiors for the Houses of Parliament, encompassing everything from ceilings to washstands. But he differed from Cole in his exclusive championing of the Gothic style as existing in spiritual and aesthetic harmony with the English character, and offering a template for resetting the foundations of society. Less concerned with markets and mass production, he believed in revealing material and construction to express essential truths and, with even more vigour than Cole, rejected superficial application of ornament on furniture, interiors and architecture. He reserved particular antipathy for illusions of depth on surfaces, whether fake architectural niches on wallpaper or naturalistic floral patterns – the latter should be geometric compositions to fill space rather than 'give a fictitious idea of relief, as if bunches of flowers were laid on'.

> The great test of Architectural beauty is the fitness of the design to the purpose for which it is intended, and it is from this that the leading ideas of any architectural arrangement must spring.
>
> Augustus Pugin, 1836

A slow burn

The devotion to flat, abstracted designs would, like many of the reformers' beliefs, later be reflected in the work of such influential figures as Owen Jones, Christopher Dresser and William Morris, but it's debatable whether design reform succeeded in its own terms. Despite their extensive involvement in the Great Exhibition, most reformers were disappointed by the floridity and variable quality on display, while popular taste continued on its different, diverse and possibly more democratic paths. The impact of their new principles was largely confined to luxury goods, rather than the mass-produced items they sought to transform.

Yet for the Great Exhibition's jury, a 'great truth' had been expressed – that 'art and taste are henceforth to be considered as elements of industry and trade, of scarcely less importance than the most powerful machinery'. It was a fundamental moment in the emergence of modern design, and of the design profession, giving design and designers a central role in industrial production and a moral weight in society that – even though it took a very long time – eventually reshaped popular tastes too.

Despite the impassioned voices decrying naturalistic forms on homewares, the market for florid wallpapers remained, and reformers were viewed with some scorn, not least by novelist Charles Dickens. In *Hard Times* (1854), which tackles industrialization, an official (a caricature of Henry Cole) delivers a stern lecture to Sissy, the young circus girl embodying both imagination and common sense: 'You are not to have, in any object of use or ornament, what would be a contradiction in fact. You don't walk upon flowers in fact; you cannot be allowed to walk upon flowers in carpets. You don't find that foreign birds and butterflies come and perch upon your crockery; you cannot be permitted to paint foreign birds and butterflies upon your crockery. . .You must use. . .for all these purposes, combinations and modifications (in primary colours) of mathematical figures which are susceptible of proof and demonstration. This is the new discovery. This is fact. This is taste.' In years to come, many Modernist designers would take Dickens's satire as a model for advancing their cause.

The condensed idea
Restoring society through design

03 The Great Exhibition

The Great Exhibition of the Works of Industry of All Nations, held in London's Hyde Park from May to October 1851, kicks off many design books, positioned as the starting point of modern design. But the precise nature of the objects displayed is often given limited attention in contrast to the structure that housed them. Dubbed the Crystal Palace by the contemporary press, this vast edifice of glass and iron is seen as pivotal to modernity – a moment at which architecture shifted from building solid mass to capturing space.

Primarily designed by horticulturalist Joseph Paxton, the world's largest building was constructed at speed and on the cheap from mass-produced, prefabricated parts. Its model was a glasshouse, with its exterior – 563m long and 33m tall (1,847 × 108ft) – covered in 300,000 of the largest panes of glass available. This mixture of lightweight, modular construction with scale and grandeur pointed to the future, to the industrialization of architecture. In decades to come, Modernist architects and designers would continually cite its importance – for its honesty in employing materials, for its otherworldliness, but also as a total expression of a building system as much as a building in its own right. As proof of that system's flexibility, as well as its more down-to-earth objectives, a barrel vault was added at the last minute, retaining existing elm trees and mollifying those angry at the despoilation of the park.

Under the vault

Despite its wonders, the Crystal Palace was intended merely as a container for the Great Exhibition's purpose, expressed in 100,000 exhibits across ten miles of display tables. These had been gathered largely at the behest of two men: Prince Albert, consort to Queen Victoria, and civil servant Henry Cole, previously involved in everything from railway gauges to postage stamps but increasingly concerned with the poor design of British manufactured goods. Denouncing the government's new school of design, he fought to establish a range of new design principles, including the balance of decorative standards and utility, the appropriateness of decoration to function, and the subservience of ornament to construction.

In an era of global trade, and with Britain's monopoly on mass production waning, a decline in exports and rise in imports were feared, with consequent impacts on the economy and employment. Holding a massive display on the sophisticated model of the French national exhibitions of the 1830s and 1840s would raise the standards of manufacture, as well as improve the taste of the public, artisans, designers and industrialists, expanding internal and external markets. After prolonged debate, Prince Albert decreed that this event was to be 'not merely national in its scope and benefits, but comprehensive of the whole world', celebrating the mutual benefits of free trade, promoting British industry to all, and offering the opportunity to learn from the best of foreign produce.

In total, 14,000 exhibitors took part, those from Britain and its 'colonies and dependencies' housed in one half of the Crystal Palace, and those from 34 'foreign states' in the other, all centred around an 8m-tall (26ft) fountain of pink glass. Exhibits were categorized as manufactures, machines, materials or fine art, with steam engines, spinning machines and steam hammers proving particularly popular. A contemporary guide detailed how 'every one may be able to see how cloth is made for his clothes, leather for boots, linen for shirts, silk for gowns, ribbons and handkerchiefs; how lace is made; how a pin and needle, a button, a knife, a sheet of paper, a ball of thread, a nail, a screw, a pair of stockings are made, how a carpet is woven.' A series of courts dedicated to Greece, Egypt, Tunisia, Assyria, India and elsewhere also proved a big draw, while the newly acquired Koh-i-Noor diamond was granted its own display space in the central gallery. And throughout were the 'manufactures' – textiles, furniture, ceramics, ironware, jewellery and more – provided by both British and foreign companies, many choosing their most flamboyant products to stand out amid the hubbub.

Brickbats and bouquets

Reactions to the Great Exhibition varied wildly, but its impact was undeniable. Over 24 weeks, it drew more than six million visitors across all social classes, including the teenage William Morris, who expressed disgust while sitting on a bench outside. Charlotte Brontë's response was more enthusiastic: 'It seems as if magic only could have gathered this mass of wealth from all the ends of the earth – as if none but supernatural hands could have arranged it thus, with such a blaze and contrast of colours and marvellous power of effect. The multitude filling the great aisles seems ruled and subdued by some invisible influence.' Queen Victoria, at the opening of her husband's tour de force, was 'filled with devotion, more so than any service I ever heard.'

Voices from the design community, including those who had helped organize the event, were generally critical, attacking the floridity, historicism and ornamentation of the machine-made products on display. Leading design reformer Owen Jones asserted that most exhibits displayed 'novelty without beauty, beauty without intelligence and all work without faith'. He turned for solace to the Indian exhibits, which showed 'all the principles, all the unity, all the truth, for which we had looked elsewhere in vain'. Art critic John Ruskin felt that the lesson to be learned from the Great Exhibition was that 'design in the hands of a machine-minded money-seeking generation tends to take a downward curve'. However, contemporary products gathered by architect Augustus Pugin for his Medieval Court came in for wide praise, in part because they evinced the moral quality that much of the exhibition lacked, and in part because they favoured abstraction over naturalism, crystallizing a trend that was to remain dominant in British design for a century or more.

> It is a wonderful place – vast, strange, new and impossible to describe. Its grandeur does not consist in one thing, but in the unique assemblage of all things. Whatever human industry has created, you find there.
>
> Charlotte Brontë, 1851

Net effects

Despite attacks on French goods from Cole's new *Journal of Design*, it remained clear that the country's long superiority in luxury manufacture remained intact. Debates began as to whether pursuing quality in both mass production and luxury markets was viable, or a certain way to fail in both, with some pointing to the strength of American and German industry as the real threat to British manufacturing. The vigour of such discussions indicates one of the Great Exhibition's achievements – the fostering of an extensive, and sometimes angry discourse around all aspects of what was now increasingly referred to as 'design', including methods of production, but even more on morals, markets and aesthetics. In tandem, the huge attendances heralded the emergence of a mass activity focused on the scrutiny and acquisition of goods. The government had, at considerable cost, staged a major exhibition to impose standards of good taste on the nation, from manufacturers to general public, and unleashed a new world of spectacle and consumerism.

The condensed idea
Design as spectacle

04 Arts and Crafts

Condemnation of industry, and its assault on nature and human dignity, was nothing new in 1887, when the Arts & Crafts Exhibition Society was founded. In the mid-19th century, however, that criticism expanded to its impact on the decorative arts too. For Richard Redgrave, a judge at London's famed Great Exhibition of the Works of Industry of All Nations in 1851, the extraordinary new machinery on display gave manufacturers 'the ability to produce the florid and overloaded as cheaply as simple forms', pandering to the debased tastes of a mass audience. The teenage William Morris – later to become the Arts & Crafts Exhibition Society's president – was blunter, calling the exhibited products 'wonderfully ugly'.

The inspiration of John Ruskin

In his early journey from aspiring clergyman to poetry, painting and eventually design, William Morris was inspired by the art critic John Ruskin. In stirring prose, Ruskin drew a direct line between the failings of industrial goods and those of industrial production, contrasting both with Gothic architecture, with its 'profound sympathy with the fullness and wealth of the material universe'. For Ruskin, the division of labour had removed the sense of achievement that came with engaging directly with materials, and from creating goods from start to finish. Endless repetitive tasks extracted joy from work, while creating hierarchies of both social classes and the arts, with decorative arts firmly positioned at the base. The result was shoddy and 'dishonest' goods, degraded lives and a diminished society, in which only the pursuit of wealth mattered.

The birth of Arts and Crafts

By the 1860s, William Morris had become the figurehead of a movement to reform the design and production of everyday objects, as well as decorative ones. He asked, 'What business have we with art at all, unless all can share it?' For Morris, as for Ruskin, the benefits of productive, pleasurable work were reflected in the quality and beauty of its output. His fear was that the potential to produce such work had been all but eroded by industry. To counter this prospect, he championed rural crafts, small workshops and the equality of the arts, while arguing that workers' conditions should be improved, and that artists should produce their own designs.

In 1861, Morris established the firm that was to become Morris & Co., producing both 'necessary work-a-day furniture' and 'state furniture', as well as textiles, stained glass and ceramics, often drawing on medieval precedents. Among its many talented designers were architects including William Burges and Philip Webb, the latter of whom also designed Morris's first home; Pre-Raphaelite painters including Ford Madox Brown and Dante Gabriel Rossetti; and Morris's daughter May, who later founded the Women's Guild of Arts. By 1877, Morris & Co. had opened its own showroom on London's Oxford Street, and four years later established its own workshop in the south of the capital, bringing together much of its manufacturing.

> Mechanical Toil will sweep over all the handiwork of man, and art will be gone.
> William Morris, 1881

Morris's views on design tended to the austere: 'Our furniture should be good citizen's furniture, solid and well made in workmanship, and in design should have nothing about it that is not easily defensible, no monstrosities or extravagances, not even of beauty, lest we weary of it'. Many of Morris & Co.'s furniture designs were modest, adapting rural typologies that possessed an aesthetic and practicality proven by time. Common materials and simple joinery were used, with the latter exposed for decorative effect. Morris himself increasingly concentrated on textile and wallpaper patterns that drew on European and Middle Eastern precursors, balancing expression and formality to reveal nature rather than imitate it.

A blunted ambition

Given their handcrafted production, the company's goods could not compete with mass-produced alternatives in price, so much of Morris's time was spent 'ministering to the swinish luxury of the rich', as he put it. Whether there was, in fact, a popular appetite for Morris & Co.'s output is open to debate – improvements in production processes meant that far greater colour and comfort were available elsewhere. As it became clear to Morris that his work was failing to

Strawberry Thief

First produced in 1883, Strawberry Thief is among the best known of William Morris's textile designs, inspired by thrushes raiding strawberries in the garden of his Oxfordshire home, Kelmscott Manor, and intended to be draped on walls or furniture, or turned into curtains. One of the most expensive cotton fabrics sold by Morris & Co., it was printed by hand with woodblocks, with costly indigo – 'the only real blue dye' according to Morris – applied via a complex bleaching method that created two different shades. Despite the cost, it proved, and remains, one of his most popular designs, formal and fluid, with its rich colours enhanced by sharp outlines.

protect craft, or bring benefits to the wider population, he gradually moved towards an acceptance of mechanization as necessary to improving people's lives, and towards socialism as a solution to society's failings.

Yet the Arts and Crafts movement had an enormous impact in Britain and beyond, inspiring a profusion of associations, schools and workshops in the late 19th and early 20th centuries, from the United States to Japan. Some, such as the Deutsche Werkbund, helped lay the path towards Modernism, embracing Morris's concern for simplicity and functionality, but coming to more complete accommodations with mass production. Others, such as the Guild and School of Handicraft, founded in London by Arts and Crafts architect C R Ashbee, stayed true to craft as both mode of production and ethical proposition, but eventually decamped to rural settings as markets and skilled labour proved elusive, turning into communities as much as manufacturers. Their decision to focus on practising and preserving craft was criticized at the time as a short-sighted refusal to engage with the modern world. A century or so later, this retreat feels rather more radical.

The condensed idea
Craft as the meeting point of art and life

05 Aestheticism

European design in the 19th century was a pretty heavy affair. Reformers in Britain believed that better education was vital to improve the quality of industrial goods, and to fight off international competition. Training the general public in good taste was also key, building a domestic market and inculcating a mutual vision for the country's future. The Arts and Crafts movement went further with this moralizing, seeing craft as emblematic of a just society, in contrast to the dehumanizing effects of mass production. Simplicity in form and honesty in materials and construction were a consequence and symbol of these deeply held beliefs.

At some point, all this seriousness was going to cause a backlash. When this came, in the 1860s, it adopted the French slogan *l'art pour l'art* – 'art for art's sake'. For the leaders of this new Aesthetic movement, the leaden nature of Victorian design was to be cast aside, as was the ugliness of industry. The moral hectoring of the Arts and Craft movement, with its over-priced armchairs, was also spurned. Instead, beauty was all. Before long, that conviction was to cross the Atlantic, and find counterparts throughout Europe.

Beauty reveals everything

The most eloquent champion of Aestheticism, until blunted by his imprisonment for 'gross indecency', was the poet and playwright Oscar Wilde. Written in 1890, his essay 'The Critic as Artist' – the nearest thing to a manifesto of the movement – opens with a powerful passage equating art with music, which concludes: 'Beauty has as many meanings as man has moods. Beauty is the symbol of symbols. Beauty reveals everything, because it expresses nothing. When it shows itself, it shows us the whole fiery-coloured world.'

The art that is frankly decorative is the art to live with.
Oscar Wilde, 1891

At this point, perhaps 30 years had passed since Aestheticism's tentative beginnings. The artists and designers associated with the movement took inspiration from myriad sources, one of which was, somewhat ironically, the Arts and Crafts movement. In large part, this was to do with Arts and Crafts' goal of bringing art into everyday life, but the undeniable beauty of its products, from the wallpapers of William Morris to the architecture of Philip Webb, also had a lot to do with it. In emotional terms, the Pre-Raphaelite movement was probably a closer sibling, with such romantically inclined artists and poets as Dante Gabriel Rossetti and Edward Burne-Jones embracing colour, nature and literature in the pursuit of truth and beauty in a manner that overlapped with the Aesthetic movement.

Other inspirations included everything from Neoclassical sculpture to Egyptian temples, but Japanese art and design was adopted with particular passion. *Ukiyo-e* prints reached Europe in the wake of the country's 'opening up' to the West in 1854, bringing a new simplicity and sophistication in their wake. They provoked admiration for their flattened perspectives, asymmetrical compositions and use of blank space, as well as such decorative details as latticework and cherry blossom. Displayed en masse with other Japanese artefacts at the 1862 International Exhibition in South Kensington, the effect was intense. A number of British architects adopted *japonisme* with enthusiam, as evidenced by Thomas Jeckyll's patterned fire surrounds bearing stylized Japanese motifs like sunflowers and dragonflies, or the ebonized wooden sideboards of E W Godwin, with pared-back rectilinear designs that still look startlingly modern today.

Even more surprising are the teapots and toast racks in electroplated silver designed by Christopher Dresser, previously associated with the design reform movement. In 1876, he was the first Western designer to tour Japan, importing the country's goods thereafter. His experiences contributed to the symmetrical, unadorned geometric forms of his tableware, which still appear almost out of time. Designed for mass production by different companies, they have gained him the title of the 'father of industrial design'.

But, if pressed to choose just one artist as the epitome of Aestheticism, it would be the American painter James McNeill Whistler, who arrived in London in 1859, having spent five hedonistic and formative years among the Parisian avant-garde. The lyrical qualities of his paintings and prints, depicting everything from nocturnal London to enigmatic full-length figures, drew on a multiplicity of sources, including Japanese prints and

Also known as Harmony in Blue and Gold, the Peacock Room is possibly the masterpiece of Aestheticism. Created in 1876 for the Kensington home of shipping magnate F R Leyland – an ardent collector of Chinese blue-and-white porcelain – it was shipped across to Detroit by industrialist Charles Lang Freer in 1904, and now lives in the Freer Gallery of Art, Washington, DC. Designer Thomas Jeckyll was commissioned to transform Leyland's dining room for the display of his collection, introducing Japanese elements such as latticework shelves, but James McNeill Whistler took over when Jeckyll fell ill in 1876, and was told to complete the project with only minor changes. It took on a life, and aesthetic, of its own. Whistler painted over Leyland's imported leather wall coverings and gilded the shelves, justifying his actions: 'I went on – without design or sketch – it grew as I painted. I reached such a point of perfection – putting in every touch with such freedom – that when I came round to the corner where I started, why, I had to paint part of it over again, as the difference would have been too marked. And the harmony in blue and gold developing, you know, I forgot everything in my joy in it!'

French Realism. They employed simple forms and muted tones, evoking a reaction akin to music – an association reflected in their titles – in contrast to the literalism of so much Victorian art.

Crossing the Atlantic

In May 1876 the Centennial International Exposition opened in Philadelphia, bringing Aestheticism to the United States, along with a 'Japan mania'. Two Japanese-inspired pavilions were exhibited, one in cast iron designed by Thomas Jeckyll, and a more traditional wood structure built by Japanese craftsmen, the latter causing 'astonishment at its beauty and elegance of finish' according to one guide. The import of Aestheticism had a similar effect on the domestic sphere, but also led to a wider embrace of contemporary art by collectors and museums, and a proliferation of art publications and societies. Its influence can be seen in the botanical-inspired stained glass of John La Farge and, in particular, Louis Comfort Tiffany, whose mesmeric windows and lamps drew on multiple sources, while remaining thoroughly contemporary. Aestheticism also permeated the Japan-inspired pottery of Maria Longworth and embroidery of Candace Wheeler, despite which women's decorative art was allotted a separate pavilion at the 1876 exposition. It can even be detected in the prairie houses of Frank Lloyd Wright decades later.

Decline and fall

By the 1880s, the Aesthetic movement had impacted on middle-class domestic life in an unprecedented fashion, filling homes with peacock-feather wallpaper, and with Chinese blue-and-white ceramics on display stands and sideboards. Aestheticism's belief in the unalloyed, ineffable truths of art lived on in the Symbolist movement in France, with founder Stéphane Mallarmé stating: 'To define is to kill. To suggest is to create.' And, with its flattened perspective and floral decoration, it helped to shape the international Art Nouveau movement. The sensitive, fragile figure of the Aesthete was the subject of affectionate parody by the 1880s, but in many ways that was indicative of a job done. If the responsibilities of art to society remain a subject of debate today, the balance of opinion falls firmly on the side of the Aesthetic movement, and its motto of 'art for art's sake'.

The condensed idea
Art for art's sake

06 Art Nouveau

I t might seem a stretch to claim that Art Nouveau – a diverse movement best known for decorative appeal – expressed one cohesive, profound idea. Yet, through its rejection of historical styles for an art focused on the senses, Art Nouveau, or 'new art', provided an essential break from the past, making design's radical reinvention in the 20th century possible. Characterized by organic forms and elaborate flourishes, the movement sought to bring together the fine and decorative arts to create beautiful (and beautifully crafted) objects, but also complete interiors that acted as *Gesamtkunstwerks* – total works of art. It achieved international reach and popular appeal, but despite – or perhaps because of – this success, Art Nouveau's critical status has always been fragile.

Founding a movement

Although known by a variety of different names at the time, La Maison d'Art Nouveau – a Paris showroom opened by Japanese art dealer Siegfried Bing in 1895 – is usually cited as the source of the movement's title. The style had been in gestation for a decade or more, evolving out of the Arts and Crafts and Aesthetic movements. In the United States, Louis Comfort Tiffany had recently started producing his sinuous blown-glass vases, with their subtle, iridescent tones, and complex stained-glass lamps and windows depicting wisteria, peacock feathers and landscape scenes. In France, Émile Gallé's opaque glass vases, with their expressive botanical forms, were equally celebrated. Both men were influenced by the recent influx of Japanese art and by avant-garde art; the wares of both were displayed at the opening of La Maison d'Art Nouveau, amid interiors designed by Henry van de Velde, later to play a formative role in the establishment of the Bauhaus.

Although he favoured more sober designs, Bing remained an important figure until his death in 1905. Alongside the fantastical work of Symbolist artists such as Félix Vallotton and Maurice Denis, he championed the darkly erotic drawings of Aubrey Beardsley and the innovative jewellery of René Lalique, with dragonflies, beetles and nymphs fashioned from semi-precious stones and translucent

Alphonse Mucha

Whether advertising cigarettes, ink or (most famously) the performances of leading lady Sarah Bernhardt, the seductive posters of the Czech artist Alphonse Mucha almost always centred on graceful women. Framed by their flowing hair, these beauties were positioned asymmetrically in botanical settings – sometimes natural landscapes, sometimes intricate patterns depicting mosaics, ironwork or glass. Mucha's treatment of colour and space echoed Japanese woodblock prints, as did the strong outlines around figures; playful hand-lettering was often integrated into the design. Despite his reluctance to be categorized as such, Mucha established himself as Art Nouveau's go-to illustrator, producing successful stand-alone series dedicated to such subjects as the seasons or precious stones, each represented by an alluring female. In 1904, he left Paris for the United States, but eventually settled in Prague to pursue his dream of creating monumental paintings dedicated to Slavic history.

enamels. Bing's pavilion, Art Nouveau Bing, was a key venue at the Exposition Universelle, held in Paris in 1900, often seen as the movement's climax, with its lavish displays of decorative arts from France and beyond.

The unity of the arts

Art Nouveau's international success had a great deal to do with another major artistic centre, Brussels. The swirling shopfronts and houses of architect Paul Hankar combined structure with decoration, bringing its style to the city's streets, but Victor Horta's Hôtel Tassel, completed in 1893, is seen as the movement's first complete expression. Architecture and design are brought together in a plethora of undulating lines suggestive of nature, movement and growth that spread across its interiors, from the central atrium's wrought-iron staircase and wall murals to the central skylight above. Hôtel Tassel had a profound effect on leading French architect Hector Guimard, as evidenced by his iconic entrances for the Paris Métro. First unveiled for the Exposition Universelle, their plant-like cast-iron frames provide both structure and aesthetic.

> **What must be avoided at all cost is the parallel and symmetry. Nature is the greatest builder of all, and nature makes nothing that is parallel and nothing that is symmetrical.**
>
> Hector Guimard

To Europe and beyond

Art Nouveau spread rapidly across Europe in the late 1890s, a dissemination facilitated by improvements in print technology. It was embraced with fervour in Eastern Europe, and in regional cities such as Darmstadt, Glasgow and Palermo adopted as a statement of confidence and prosperity. Similarly, it flourished in Central and South American capitals, expressing modernity and independence. Particularly influential were the designs of Glasgow architect Charles Rennie Mackintosh, with his more geometric approach, as well as the work of the Vienna Secession, whose members included Josef Hoffmann and Gustav Klimt, and that of Munich's Jugendstil (youth style) movement. One of the latter's founders, August Endell, proclaimed the advent of a 'totally new art. . .with forms that mean nothing and represent nothing and recall nothing'. The term 'whiplash' was first applied to intertwined cyclamen stems in a tapestry by his friend Hermann Obrist, and soon became the go-to description for the S-shaped lines that provided a visual trademark for the movement.

Art Nouveau's legacy

By the start of World War I, Art Nouveau's popularity had waned. Fashions had moved on, with sleek forms that engaged with the possibilities of industrial production pushing aside its impractical, expensive and often handmade products. Many Art Nouveau designers – including another Jugendstil designer, Peter Behrens, and many members of the Vienna Secession – shifted towards rectilinearity and an incipient Modernism. Art Nouveau dropped out of design literature for decades, perceived as a decadent last fling for the 19th century's decorative excess, lacking Modernism's intellectual and aesthetic rigour. In the 1960s, however, it started to creep back in through retrospective exhibitions, trendy boutiques and psychedelic designs, as well as the endless reproductions of its enchanting posters that have adorned student accommodation ever since. This endurance suggests that this totally new art 'runs deep into our souls, so deeply and so strongly as only music can do', just as August Endell declared.

The condensed idea
Nature and nothing more

07 Scientific Management

The origins of modern design are often traced, with good reason, to the Industrial Revolution and the mechanization of production. But the journey from introducing machines to the factory floor to 'mass production' was long and complex, requiring innovation across multiple spheres, including architecture, engineering, transport, industrial relations, design and management – and, in particular, 'scientific management', which fostered the standardization, consistency and affordability that unlocked industrial design.

Taking control

In 1911, Frederick Winslow Taylor published *The Principles of Scientific Management*, a book drawing on his experiences as a machinist, and then a manager, at the Midvale Steel Company in Nicetown, Pennsylvania, and then at a steel works at Bethlehem. Encountering inconsistency in both organization and output, and observing what he believed to be 'soldiering' – workers deliberately minimizing effort over time – he undertook a series of experiments, spread over decades, aimed at developing better ways of working. Most effective were time-and-motion studies breaking each task down to its simplest elements and measuring how long these took to perform, and the motions involved in each, to discover the most efficient ways in which they could be performed. In addition, he trialled different factory layouts, feed rates, handling techniques and tool sizes and shapes in pursuit of options that would save time and energy, while reducing wear and tear on workers and machines alike. Once determined, these approved methods could then be taught to suitable employees, with the roles of managers and workers strictly separated. The former would 'scientifically' plan the work and conduct ongoing tests in a 'planning department', while the latter would be confined to, and trained for, specific roles, picking up their daily instructions and targets and following new methods scrupulously, thus removing 'all possible brain work' from the factory floor.

Taylor's recommendations were, in the eyes of many, dehumanizing, resulting in repetitive, de-skilled jobs with little possibility of creativity or advancement. It did not help that his extensive experimentation with piece-rate systems also led him to advocate vigorously for workers' pay to directly reflect their output. He defended his stance by saying that '[t]he principal object of management

In the past the man has been first; in the future the system must be first.
Frederick Winslow Taylor, 1911

should be to secure the maximum prosperity for the employer, coupled with the maximum prosperity of each employee.' Through increased productivity, he believed that the salaries of all would inevitably be increased, and a harmonious, thriving workplace created in which everyone knew, and was well trained in, their specific roles.

Tellingly, an attempt to impose scientific management on workers at the US Army's Watertown Arsenal in Massachusetts in 1911 resulted in protests and a walkout, with a letter of complaint stating: 'It is humiliating to us, who have always tried to give to the Government the best that was in us. This method is un-American in principle.' A congressional investigation was convened, at which Taylor's own defence of his principles proved counter-productive. When asked what happened to those workers not classed 'first rate' in his system, he simply replied: 'Scientific management has no place for a bird that can sing and won't sing.' The result was its removal at Watertown, and the restriction of time-and-motion studies in government service. Contemporary proponents of the theories took such criticisms on board, however, with Frank and Lillian Gilbreth introducing a greater focus on psychology, as well as looking at the ergonomic and efficient performance of 17 specific actions known as 'therbligs' (a play on their name), aided by the introduction of still- and motion-picture cameras.

Management in motion

An instant bestseller – a first for a business book – *The Principles of Scientific Management* was so influential that its tenets would come to be known simply as 'Taylorism' – but they were soon joined by 'Fordism'. In 1913, automobile magnate Henry Ford instituted his pioneering assembly line at Highland Park, Michigan, to meet demand for his new Model T. Bringing together existing systems of conveyor belts and overhead pulleys, with the vehicle hauled down the line by a moving-chain mechanism, he created a production line that minimized time wasted in moving components from one workstation to another. Following Taylor's example, Ford made extensive use of time-and-motion studies, while also expanding the division of labour. However, Ford rejected piece work in favour of a generous fixed wage, believing that, by rewarding speed alone, the former threatened to undermine the consistent quality that he needed, while also aggravating workers. Overall, the results were dramatic, with each Model T assembled in only 90 minutes, and prices diving from $825 in 1908 to $260 in 1925 – the last one rolled off the production line two years later.

Crossing the Atlantic

Scientific management went international quickly, with Taylor's book also published in France in 1911. Time-and-motion studies were held at Renault's factories immediately, with strikes against reduced piece rates the following year. Although Michelin had already introduced

The Frankfurt Kitchen

In the late 1920s, Frankfurt was a hotbed of Modernist architects. Among them was Margarete 'Grete' Schütte-Lihotzky, who designed the so-called Frankfurt Kitchen for the city's new social-housing estates, with 10,000 eventually installed. A masterclass in efficient design, it was the first fully realized fitted kitchen, and drew heavily on scientific management to analyse how the restricted space available could best be used. Schütte-Lihotzky ran extensive time-and-motion studies, prompting such innovations as hinged ironing boards, wipe-clean surfaces and easy-to-reach storage containers, with the goal of freeing up time to allow women to both socialize and go out to work. But, just like Taylor's factories, the new kitchens were criticized for creating dehumanizing environments, particularly those with galley layouts that trapped women in a small niche with a sliding door while the promised social life went on elsewhere. Although many of Schütte-Lihotzky's innovations remain in use, today the open-plan layout reigns supreme.

stopwatches to its tyre factories four years earlier, it proved less wholehearted about the new practices. But in 1921, as France struggled with reduced workforces in the wake of World War I, the Comité Michelin was founded to disseminate Taylor's ideas across the country. More surprisingly, after some initial scepticism, Lenin proved an advocate for their implementation in Soviet Russia, finding synergies between the principles of scientific management and those of planned economies, stating in 1919: 'The possibility of Socialism will be determined by our success in combining Soviet organization and management with the latest progressive measures of capitalism. We must introduce in Russia the study and teaching of the Taylor school and its systematic trial and adoption.' American industrial advisors were soon invited to Moscow.

Scientific management's time in the sun didn't last, replaced by more agile, creative and egalitarian approaches pioneered in Japan in the 1950s. Its fading was perhaps inevitable at a time of such rapid industrial change, and Taylor's misjudgement of human psychology was fundamental. Yet his principles reshaped the manufacturing process, in both concept and practice. This new system of work was a sophisticated piece of design in its own right, while also facilitating the rise of Modernism, and all the chrome chairs to come.

The condensed idea
Designing for productivity

08 Art Deco

When reading surveys of 20th-century design, it's always interesting to see where Art Deco crops up. The movement is pretty much contemporaneous with Modernism, so some authors get it out of the way first, presenting it as a more orderly successor to Art Nouveau – essentially a decorative arts movement rather than true design. Others tackle it briefly afterwards – a superficial sibling to Modernism, overlapping in aesthetics and personnel, but with a focus on ornament and luxury rather than changing the world. In both scenarios, its secondary importance is assumed, despite its huge popularity then and since.

Choosing a name

The name 'Art Deco' only gained currency in the 1960s, deriving from the massive Exposition internationale des arts décoratifs et industriels modernes (International Exhibition of Modern Decorative and Industrial Arts) held in Paris in 1925. At the time, '*style moderne*' and '*art moderne*' were more common, with words such as 'jazz' or 'zigzag' substituted when appropriate motifs appeared. This lack of a firm title was in part due to the highly eclectic nature of the movement's influences and outputs. Its use of natural ornament and strong outlines drew on Art Nouveau, but these were employed in a more abstract fashion, with the patterns flattened and elongated to create striking geometric forms. Neoclassical furniture and decoration provided a rich source of inspiration, particularly for the more luxurious end of the market, while the dramatic discovery of Tutankhamun's tomb in the Valley of the Kings, in November 1922, resulted in a proliferation of scarabs, hieroglyphics, pylons and pyramids, sometimes mixed with Babylonian, Aztec and African motifs, or with sunbursts and lightning bolts, in an arbitrary and occasionally racist fashion. In friezes, murals and sculptures, sensuous depictions of the human form were mandatory.

> Whether you want it or not, a style is just a craze. And fashion does not come up from humble backgrounds.
>
> Émile-Jacques Ruhlmann, 1920

Making an entrance

When the Exposition internationale opened in 1925, sprawling across both banks of the Seine and attracting 16 million visitors, it was clear that a new modernity was being expressed, although not perhaps the one organizers envisaged. Seeking a response to the simple, affordable goods being manufactured by German industry, the event's brief specifically rejected historical styles, stating that products should show 'clearly modern tendencies' and reflect 'new modes of living', arguing that 'everyday objects are as capable of being beautiful as the most exclusive objects'. The reality was somewhat different. The occasion was seized upon by exhibitors to restate France's long-standing pre-eminence in the decorative arts, so luxury, craftsmanship and historicism dominated.

Although two major Modernist statements did infiltrate the exhibition site – the jagged Soviet Pavilion by Constructivist architect Konstantin Melnikov and Le Corbusier's prefabricated Pavillon de L'Esprit Nouveau – the most popular pavilions were those erected by leading French manufacturers and department stores. Ceramics firm Sèvres commissioned a glass dining room from erstwhile jeweller René Lalique for its exotic concrete temple designed by architect Pierre Patout, while Parisian department store Galeries Lafayette adorned its imposing octagon pavilion, dedicated to 'the current renaissance of the applied arts', with an impressive stained-glass sunburst by Jacques Grüber. However, Art Deco's splendour was best captured by the Hôtel d'un Collectionneur, also by Patout. Inside, the elegant suite of rooms was largely dedicated to the handcrafted Neoclassical furniture of Émile-Jacques Ruhlmann, which combined extravagant materials – many imported from French colonies – with restrained forms to immaculate effect. Ruhlmann's attitude to his work provided a provocative, and honest, summation of the real priorities of the Exposition internationale: 'Along with satisfying a desire for change, fashion's real purpose is to display wealth.'

Global impacts

However, Art Deco did spread rapidly, both around the globe – with particular vigour in Argentina and the United States – and through social classes, encountered in cinema foyers and department store lifts, and as perfume bottles, dinnerware, cigarette cases, fireplaces or

Art Deco afloat

When it came to styling some of the largest and most beautiful machines of the interwar years, shipping companies turned to the elegance of Art Deco. The SS *Normandie* was the greatest liner of the age, subsidized by the French government to champion the country's engineering and craftsmanship, and drawing on the design talent that had erupted at the 1925 Exposition internationale. Its ambition and extravagance were exemplified by the first-class dining room, modelled on, but significantly longer than, the Hall of Mirrors at Versailles. Designed by Art Deco's premier architect, Pierre Patout, this extraordinary space rose through three decks, seated seven hundred and featured massive glass chandeliers and 'firepots' by Lalique, all presided over by a huge, if somewhat insipid, bronze

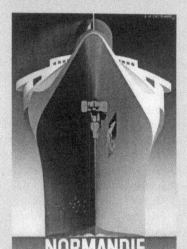

figure of peace by Louis Dejean. In 1942, the SS *Normandie* caught fire and sank in New York Harbor while being refitted as a troop ship, bringing the curtain down on the Art Deco era. The iconic poster of the approaching liner's looming prow, commissioned from graphic designer A M Cassandre to mark her first voyage, is fitting tribute to both the ship and the style.

radio sets. Transport companies proved particularly keen, with Lalique commissioned to provide sumptuous frosted-glass dividers for the luxurious Côte d'Azur Pullman Express train service. Art Deco architects, designers and manufacturers also engaged in astute collaborations with, and adaptations from, contemporary artists, bringing Cubist and Futurist aesthetics to wide audiences. As its popularity grew in the 1930s, Art Deco became increasingly geometrical in character and new materials were exploited – as much for their decorative as their practical qualities – with emergent plastics such as Bakelite taking the place of tortoiseshell or ivory.

Despite consistent criticism of Art Deco as kitsch and superficial, and negative comparisons to Modernism's commitment to standardization and social progress, for huge audiences at the time its outputs clearly did express the intense nature of contemporary life. They communicated a vision of modernity that rang true – one of travel, speed, advertising, entertainment, wit and excitement – capturing the imagination and bringing pleasure in a manner Modernist design rarely achieved. Art Deco's huge popularity today suggests that this still holds true.

The condensed idea
Celebrating the excitement and possibility of modern life

09 Industrial Design

Debates around the beginnings of industrial design are messy. Peter Behrens is often hailed as the first fully fledged industrial designer for his work at German electrical manufacturer Allgemeine Elektricitäts-Gesellschaft (AEG) from 1907, although the term itself was wasn't coined until 12 years later. The long delay between the advent of mass production and that of industrial design indicates just how slow designers and industrialists were to realize their shared future, and the mutual benefits it would bring. For members of the Arts and Crafts movement in the late 19th century, the dubious quality and aesthetics of machine-made products, as well as the social and environmental damage caused by their manufacture, provided a strong reason to resist rather than embrace collaboration with industry.

Embracing mass production

For some, however, mass production was an opportunity. In the early 20th century, Modernist designers in Europe started to adopt standardization as a means to create products and families of products that could be manufactured cheaply and quickly to a high quality, making good design available to a wide section of the population. These 'universal designs', timeless in their aesthetics and practicality, would improve lives and tastes, helping to forge a new society. In practice, however, introducing new forms and innovative materials often involved expensive handcrafted production, and designs that many found alien, restricting markets for the final products.

A less idealistic strand of industrial design arrived with the economic gloom of the 1930s. American corporations, saddled with expensive manufacturing infrastructure, turned to design as a means to increase revenues. Consultants such as Henry Dreyfuss, Raymond Loewy and Norman Bel Geddes worked in collaboration with engineers, marketing departments, suppliers and financiers to design affordable, attractive goods that would excite consumers. Famously, Harley Earl introduced annual updates, largely cosmetic, to General Motors' automobile ranges to make cars from previous years appear unfashionable, hastening their disposal for the latest model. Some products of the era endured, such as Dreyfuss's Bakelite phones for the Bell Telephone Company, or Walter Dorwin Teague's lightweight cameras for Kodak. Often, however, the focus was on styling items to stimulate demand with minimal outlay, providing streamlined cladding for the era's technological innovations.

This single-minded approach might seem less praiseworthy than universal design, but it could also claim to be more effective in improving lives, making consumer goods accessible to wider segments of society. When justifying the tactic, however, American commentators put a greater emphasis on its role in increasing sales of goods, driving profitability and providing employment, describing this 'creative waste' as a means to national prosperity. The drawbacks of a throwaway society were only just being recognized and are still being tackled today.

> There is only one reason for hiring an industrial designer, and that is to increase sales of a product.
> Designer J Gordon Lippincott, 1947

A cult of design

Despite the glamour that attached itself to this new breed of American designers, it was the European tradition, and in particular the Bauhaus, that received greater recognition from such authorities as the Museum of Modern Art, New York. Founded in 1929, the institution held its inaugural design exhibition five years later, displaying products by Le Corbusier and Mies van der Rohe to demonstrate that 'industrial design is functionally motivated and follows the same principles as modern architecture: machine-like simplicity, smoothness of surface, avoidance of ornament'. By the 1950s, this austere approach was being championed by a growing number of national and professional bodies, as well as by influential design magazines and college faculties, the latter often staffed by ex-Bauhaus students and teachers. Companies began to employ powerful in-house figures such as Dieter Rams at Braun and Ettore Sottsass at Olivetti, or hire external consultants such as Charles and Ray Eames and Vico Magistretti, to benefit from this compelling design philosophy and its associated aesthetics.

The discrepancy between the profession's elevated status in the post-war period, and the realities of its capitalist function and the

Designing Wedgwood

Industrial entrepreneur Josiah Wedgwood was a serial inventor and innovator, experimenting with materials and processes in his Staffordshire potteries, while using new marketing and distributing methods to get the results into the hands of consumers. Having developed a smooth, consistent creamware for his ceramics in the 1760s, he reduced the number and complexity of their shapes, speeding production and allowing increased use of moulds rather than potters' wheels. Such simple, regular forms aligned with contemporary Neoclassical tastes, but could also be decorated with a variety of different patterns, often chosen by the customer from the latest range and applied via cheap transfer-printing rather than hand-painting. A diversity of products at various price points could therefore be showcased in catalogues and showrooms, but not held as finished stock. Various processes – from modelling and mould-making to decorating and engraving – were separated, creating a rudimentary assembly line, while fashionable London artists were commissioned to design models for more flamboyant vases and reliefs. For some commentators, Wedgwood's embryonic industrial-design system reveals that the most important person in the room may not, in fact, be the designer.

associated environmental harm, was increasingly pointed out during the 1970s. The word 'industrial' began to drift from the job description as both ecology and Postmodernism made an association with art and creativity more advantageous. Yet design's relationship with mass-production remains its most important one. Working for a large corporation increases resources and impact, but comes with restrictions to creative freedom, with established production lines, systems and employees, as well as existing materials, suppliers and markets, all creating strict trammels within which the design must be realized. It is the task of the industrial designer to build the many collaborations needed to guide new ideas, technologies and products into the world, despite having little control over wider processes and ideologies – and it remains a vital one.

The condensed idea
Harnessing industrial processes to improve life

10 Mingei

Studio pottery, handmade in small batches from clay to kiln, has roots in the Arts and Crafts movement, but came of age in the 1920s with the Mingei movement, in Japan. Taking its name from the phrase *minshuteki kogei*, or ordinary people's craft, Mingei found inspiration in practical items that its founders saw being handmade in great quantities across Japan, whether textiles, tools, dolls or pots. Humble, anonymous, cheap, beautiful – and gaining additional beauty through use – these utilitarian products were 'ignored in the flow of time, because they are considered low and common', in the words of Mingei's founding intellect Yanagi Soetsu. In particular, a new appreciation of the qualities of everyday ceramics fomented a revolution in studio pottery. Natural glazes and unglazed clay were embraced, in combination with traditional forms, skills and processes, overturning conceptions of beauty that had dominated the decorative arts for centuries, particularly in Europe and the United States.

Redefining beauty

Born in Tokyo, in 1889, Soetsu was a cultural polymath at a young age, collecting traditional craft from China, Korea and Japan. He explored the art of Post-Impressionists such as Vincent van Gogh and Paul Gaugin, as well as work by William Blake, William Morris and others, extending their profile in Japan as editor of arts magazine *Shirakaba*. Disillusioned with rapid industrialization, and with machine-made products that had 'fallen victim to commercialism and the profit motive', Soetsu discovered a new artistic vision when visiting Korea in 1916. He fell under the spell of the everyday crafts he encountered, praising their innate beauty, flowing lines and monochrome finishes, famously ascribing to them 'the beauty of sadness' in reference to the country's difficult history, culminating in its annexation by Japan in 1910. Soetsu's admiration for Korean craft, and its people's 'amazing insight into the secrets of beauty', led to his role in establishing the National Folk Museum, Seoul, in 1924.

> The world of folk art is a world of freedom, a state of imaginative creation.
>
> Yanagi Soetsu, 1926

Founding Mingei

Believing Japan to be at a moment of radical change that allowed everything, including ordinary items, to be perceived afresh, Soetsu built an extensive and influential collection of regional ceramics, lacquerware and textiles. With his friends and collaborators – Bernard Leach, a British potter and teacher who lived in Toyko in the 1910s; the potter Shōji Hamada, destined to become internationally famous for his use of local materials and techniques; and the potter Kawai Kanjirō, with his eclectic exploration of modernity and tradition – Soetsu evolved the philosophies behind Mingei, coining the name by 1925. Following a series of energetic exhibitions in museums and stores, he founded the magazine *Kogei* (Crafts) and the Japan Folk Crafts Association in 1931. Five years later, the long-planned Japan Folk Crafts Museum opened, confirming this new movement as a significant cultural force in Japan.

Its vision was essentially a romantic one, celebrating the intimate relationship between rural artisans and their materials, landscapes and communities, unsullied by commerce or fame. In many ways, Mingei echoed the ideals of William Morris, who championed the handmade and '[t]he art of making beautifully all kinds of ordinary things. . .unconsciously and without effort'. Drawing on his Buddhist beliefs, Soetsu believed that a repetitive process ensured proficiency, but also artistry: 'Without consciously thinking whether something is good or bad, creating as if it were the most natural thing in the world to do, making things that are plain and simple but marvellous, this is the state of mind in which artisans do their finest work.' Without ego, without self-consciousness, these artisans were creating objects that were authentic and exquisite, providing a template for the future of Japan's arts.

In intention, Mingei was essentially apolitical, dedicated to the beauty and artistry of everyday crafts. However, it helped to preserve these crafts, many of them under threat from industrialization, many of them practised by women and ethnic minorities. Soetsu promoted their wares fervently in print and exhibitions, while creating networks for distribution and sale, aiding both practitioners and communities. He also argued that rural production could be the basis of a 'provincial industry' on a cooperative model, with new objects adapted for modern lifestyles – even if artists would be needed to provide inspiration to prevent artisans 'wandering in the dark'. Perhaps less tangibly, Mingei created a greater appreciation of the skills involved in the creation of seemingly humble items, emphasizing the close connections between object and maker, but also the important place that the ordinary still held in modern life.

Contested legacies

The reputation of Mingei has come under harsh scrutiny in recent years. Soetsu's depiction of rural industry can be jarring – for instance, his description of 'ingenuous artisans possessing no artistic ambition, without intellectual pride, soft-spoken, and happy to be leading poor but honest lives'. The dehumanizing nature of repetitive labour is ignored, while any artistry is ascribed to 'a kind of unconscious grace'. Similarly, the sophistication of rural manufacture and trade networks were overlooked, with their complex impacts on class structures, economic relationships and access to raw materials.

More damaging, however, are claims of appropriation. Mingei's advocates praised the 'creative honesty' of anonymity, repetition and tradition in poor communities in rural Japan, then employed those very traditions – and their stamp of authenticity – to create unique pieces of studio pottery for collectors. When praising the folk art of Osaka and Hokkaido – both annexed by Japan in the late 19th century

– the ongoing destruction of indigenous cultures, languages and even craft was disregarded, while Soetsu's poetic notion of the 'beauty of sorrow' in Korean craft has been condemned as an extreme simplification, employing colonial language to assign a pre-modern innocence to a country's culture.

From studio to factory

By the 1950s, Mingei had an international reputation, with Yanagi, Hamada and Leach undertaking a coast-to-coast tour of the United States in 1952, including a two-week seminar at the Bauhaus-inspired Black Mountain College in North Carolina. During the tour, their meeting with Puebloan ceramicist Maria Martinez helped extend the language of studio pottery in the United States, while similar synergies with indigenous crafts were felt in India, Canada, New Zealand and beyond. An obvious intersection with the materiality of Scandinavian design led to a major exhibition of Japanese crafts in Sweden in 1957, while, in Britain, the studio pottery established in 1920 by Leach and Hamada in St Ives is still active today.

In Japan, the movement's success resulted in efforts to introduce its ethos into factories, including the promotion of 'Japanese modern' as a synthesis of craft sensibilities, modern design and mass production. The warmth and simplicity of the Butterfly Stool designed in 1954 by Soetsu's son Sori Yanagi – two graceful curves of moulded plywood – expresses this synthesis, suggesting that Soetsu's goal of improving aesthetic standards was, in part, achieved. Without Mingei, however, it is unquestionable that the practice, ethos and aesthetics of contemporary craft would be very different.

The condensed idea
Beauty in the everyday

11 Deutscher Werkbund

t may not have the familiarity or glamour of the Bauhaus, but many would credit the Deutscher Werkbund – literally German Work Federation – as key to the emergence of modern industrial design. Established in Munich in 1907, it sought to unite artists and manufacturers to strengthen German design and industry, and together to develop mass-produced goods that would express 'the dignity and calm endeavour of a new, confident national German spirit', in the words of founder Hermann Muthesius.

Shaping modernity

Muthesius had practised as an architect in Tokyo for four years from 1887, then was attached to the German Embassy in London from 1896, resulting in his famous three-volume book on 19th-century English domestic architecture, *Das englische Haus*. His encounters with Japanese craft and design, and with the British Arts and Crafts movement, inspired him to champion simplicity and functionality as key to product design. However, he didn't share William Morris's ambivalence towards industrialization, believing that – with appropriate input from designers – attractive, affordable modern items could be mass produced, expanding Germany's internal and export markets, boosting its economy, and improving the taste of its consumers. Such was the vigour of his support for standardization, and his attacks on the quality and historical styling of current German goods, that he attracted the ire of the country's leading Arts and Crafts organization for a particularly combative lecture in 1907. The fallout, known as the 'Muthesius Affair', resulted in his role in the formation of the breakaway Deutscher Werkbund, comprising progressive designers, artists, manufacturers and even politicians, as a 'rallying point for all those who are able and willing to work for high quality'.

This goal of developing products suitable for mass production by Germany's expanding industrial base drew on mutual self-interest, but also reflected the belief that society and culture would benefit from this reform process. Under the motto '*Vom Sofakissen zum Städtebau*' (From sofa cushions to city-building), the education of both prospective designers and the general public was fostered, with exhibitions, publications and courses, along with shop-window competitions and a short-lived museum in Hagen, near Dortmund, contrasting good and bad design.

The success of the Deutscher Werkbund inspired or reinvigorated similar groups in France, Sweden, Britain and elsewhere, but tensions soon emerged between the pursuit of products adapted to industrial manufacture – affordable, durable and functional, with minimal decoration – and the desire for creative freedom. Another of the founders, the Belgian architect Henry van de Velde with a background in the Art Nouveau–inclined Jugendstil movement, argued that, rather than bowing to the lowest common denominators of industry and profit, 'art must conquer the machine'. In addition, he believed patronage had an important role to play in fashioning and guiding taste, as it had for the Arts and Crafts movement. The clash came to a head at a gathering in Cologne in 1914, when Muthesius argued for the development of product types as a means to international competitiveness and improved taste, in place of stylistic extravagance and one-offs. The proposal was badly received by most, but rupture was avoided by war.

Designing an identity

In 1907, another of the Deutscher Werkbund's co-founders – struggling artist-turned-architect Peter Behrens – was appointed by market-leading electrical company Allgemeine Elektricitäts-Gesellschaft (AEG) as 'artistic consultant', as it sought to consolidate its dominant position while power networks spread across Germany. Benefiting from the lack of precedents, Behrens was able to produce lucid modern designs for its industrial and domestic products, including kettles, lamps, fans, clocks, heaters and more. Combining standardized parts with diverse finishes provided consumers with choice in a cost-efficient manner, while giving the company's products a consistent style – one that aspired to beauty within the constraints imposed by production processes. Behrens also designed layouts and a typeface for AEG's

> Design is not about decorating functional forms – it is about creating forms that accord with the character of the object and show new technologies to advantage.
> Peter Behrens, c. 1910

advertising and catalogues, as well as a hexagonal trademark resembling a beehive, in place of its previous Art Nouveau logo. AEG is often cited as among the first companies to adopt a corporate identity, and Behrens as the first industrial designer. Their collaboration extended to AEG's stores, its staff housing and even its monumental turbine factory in central Berlin, a temple of industry with steel girders marching down each flank, expanses of reinforced concrete and glass, and the AEG logo imprinted on its facade.

Handing the baton

Henry van de Velde's return to Belgium during World War I, and the increasing focus on protecting German industry at a time of economic crisis, ensured that the 'rational' gained in appeal after defeat. Modest, well-produced everyday goods seemed appropriate to the modern

Fan GB1

Some of Behrens's consumer products for AEG can look clumsy to modern eyes. Despite the use of standardized components, their forms were often decorative, even traditional, while finishes were intended to give the impression of handcrafting, as with the mouldings and woven cane handles used for kettles. One clear exception is his Fan GB1, designed in 1908, which combines a painted cast-iron base that speaks of its industrial origins with brass fan blades to eye-catching effect, turning the utilitarian into the dramatic. Based on existing components, at first glance Fan GB1 may not seem to herald a design revolution, but its rational origins signify both its attraction and its importance.

lifestyles that would contribute to national rebuilding, unlike the waste and anachronism of ornament – it became increasingly clear that society, and its requirements, had undergone a fundamental change. However, in both practical and artistic terms, the Deutscher Werkbund was gradually being overtaken by the clarity of the Bauhaus, and it eventually disbanded in 1934 as the economic and political situations grew more oppressive.

Two major exhibitions in the 1920s left a significant mark. In 1924, the travelling *Form ohne Ornament* (Form without Ornament) displayed both machine- and craft-produced goods that eschewed historical styles in favour of simplicity and quality. These met with significant praise for exemplifying good, anonymous design. In 1927, *Die Wohnung* (The Dwelling) in Stuttgart was an important stepping stone for Modernism, including a model housing estate constructed under the guidance of the Werkbund vice president Mies van der Rohe. Here, 16 leading avant-garde architects, including Le Corbusier, Walter Gropius and Behrens, designed Modernist housing units, complete with furniture and fittings. The estate met with hostility from cultural and commercial voices threatened by its radicalism. Even Muthesius attacked the result, believing that the worship of 'the new Form' was having a 'tyrannical effect', outweighing all other considerations of practicality and economy. It turned out that the relationship between rationality and Modernism was not always going to be clear cut.

The condensed idea
New forms and improved lives

12 Modernism

Almost all the ideas in this book are, in one way or another, related to Modernism – its predecessors, progenitors, protagonists, antagonists, offshoots, outcomes and impact. Even so, they only cover those aspects of Modernism's myriad faces that overlap directly with design – the novels of Virginia Woolf, the music of Arnold Schoenberg and the art of Pablo Picasso, and much more, are encompassed within Modernism's remit. However, none of these artists – or their contemporaries within this book – would have recognized their work as such. The term 'modernism' barely existed, and neither did the notion of one single overarching movement embracing all their priorities. Yet something still bound these pioneers together.

Changing the world

In its earliest iterations – Futurism, Constructivism and Dada – Modernism embraced technology in a manner that was passionate, even delirious, seeking to sweep away all that was old in the arts and society. The trauma of World War I had ripped apart faith in the existing structures of society, and the grand narratives that had shaped them, with their presumptions of inexorable progress. Existing cultures – artistic and political – now seemed inadequate, and powerful alternatives were needed to replace them. In the war's disastrous aftermath, however, the immediate human needs of a fractured Europe became increasingly evident. The Modernist approach gradually shifted from disruption to rationalism, and a belief that through industrial production a just, egalitarian society could be achieved.

> There is a new spirit abroad: it is a spirit of construction and synthesis, moved by a clear conception of things. Whatever one may think of it, this spirit animates the greater part of human activity. . .A great epoch has begun.
> Le Corbusier, 1920

From this perspective, the machine – for the Futurists, a means to radical, total and sometimes violent transformation – became instead a practical tool to improve lives, in spiritual, material, political and social terms. Initially expressive and artistic in their output, Modernist groupings increasingly sought to engage directly with industry, and employ a unity of the arts to increase their impact while doing so. Despite retaining their utopian aspirations, there was a new acknowledgement that gradual yet sustained progress would deliver much-needed and more immediate change across society, and these groups wanted to be active and innovative participants in that process.

Given Modernism's avant-garde opinions and aesthetics, opportunities to build major projects were few in 1920s Europe, thus designing objects intended for industrial production – whether chairs, lighting, textiles or ashtrays – became a major outlet for architects' talents. If optimized and standardized for mass production, such items would be affordable and functional for all – they would be universal and classless. This vision was accompanied by various corollaries. Industrial production was (in theory at least) well matched to new materials such as tubular steel, chrome and plywood, which were light, durable, hygienic and, importantly, spoke of the future rather than the past in their aesthetics. Similarly, replacing ornament with geometry and applying the principles of 'truth to materials' and 'form follows function' – the latter first recorded in the writings of American architect Louis Sullivan in the 1890s – would inevitably result in a modern purity of form. With its timeless and abstract qualities, this new simplicity was an abiding Modernist goal – even if it found few takers among consumers at the time – and it remains wrapped up in our conceptions of the movement today.

Different yet the same

Even within progressive European circles, there was an inevitable diversity of ideology, aesthetics and audiences in the 1920s and 1930s. Some Modernist designers achieved their ambitions to deliver projects that brought about social good, from Margarete Schütte-Lihotzky's Frankfurt Kitchen to Alvar Aalto's Paimio Sanatorium. Others, such as Le Corbusier, Charlotte Perriand and Eileen Gray, catered largely to private individuals – cultured, artistic, progressive and rich. Often, the result was a style that existed somewhere between Art Deco and Modernism, in which explorations of material and form translated not into functional simplicity, but into sculptural objects that were beautiful, avant-garde and expensive. In Scandinavia, on the other hand, a more craft-oriented, soft-edged Modernism making use of natural materials offered a warm, domestic alternative to the chrome of the continent, paving the way towards the Mid-century Modernism of the 1950s. Yet, despite these differences, those in Modernist circles across Europe were aware that they were all speaking the same language – one encompassing universal values, the potential of the machine, and the rejection of the past in order to seek better futures.

Paradise lost

By the 1950s, much of Modernism's radical edge and utopian ambition had drifted away. In most countries, its protagonists had become the establishment, respected, professional, well-to-do, and deeply engaged in promoting the economies and reputations of their respective nations. 'Modernism' had now emerged as the dominant term, yet the ideals were muddier, with corporate, commercial and institutional interests paramount, rather than the pursuit of social change. Never completely successful in winning over popular affection, Modernist design's new status gradually alienated a section of younger designers too. As faith in technology as a force for positive change dwindled in the 1970s, accusations of inhumanity and ecological arrogance followed. Those charges still linger today, yet almost all the products around us retain the imprint of Modernist thinking. And, despite all its complexities and contradictions, Modernism's ideals, placing the betterment of society above all else, are still very relevant, and still have the power to move, and to inspire.

The condensed idea
Building a new world

13 Futurism

Although the short-lived flame of Futurism burned strongest in Italy, it created sparks across the world, each one controversial, each one fiercely independent, yet all united in a violent rejection of the past. Tradition was not merely to be critiqued for constraining artistic freedom, but condemned as an oppressor and overthrown in favour of modernity, technology and industry. This revolutionary credo built its greatest momentum in the years leading up to World War I, but its impacts were felt long after.

Sweeping away the past

Futurism announced itself in early 1909 with a manifesto written by the Italian poet Filippo Tommaso Marinetti, which appeared first in Italy's *La Gazzetta dell'Emilia* and shortly afterwards on the front page of France's mass-market *Le Figaro*. It demanded the sweeping away of the tradition of gatekeeping across artforms – visual, literary, musical and dramatic – that were particularly virulent in Italy, claiming that 'ruinous and incendiary violence' was justified in order 'to deliver Italy from its gangrene of professors, archaeologists, tourist guides and antiquaries'. Marinetti claimed to have been set on this Futurist course when crashing his car into a ditch as he swerved to avoid a cyclist – a symbolic clash of the old and the new, in which the old stymied the modern. Confronted by the belated industrialization of Italian cities, he called for a new art to capture this emerging urban life – its workshops, factories, aeroplanes, automobiles and crowds – in all its violent dynamism. In this purging of nostalgia, the manifesto proclaimed war as 'the only cure for the world', and also its support for 'patriotism, the destructive gesture of the anarchists, the beautiful ideas that kill'.

Word and image

It was a radical message that quickly attracted artistic disciples in Italy's cultural centres, notably Milan, Turin and Naples. Many drew on Post-Impressionism and Cubist imagery, but also on time-lapse photographs, to evoke movement and speed, in designs that featured repetition, blurring and 'lines of force'. If Marinetti provided the intellectual heft, Futurism's artistic leader proved to be Umberto Boccioni. His early masterpiece, *The City Rises*, exhibited in 1911 at the group's first major public show in Milan, depicts muscular horses surging across the foreground, with a scaffolding-clad cityscape behind.

Marinetti soon took the group's message to Paris, Berlin, London, Brussels and other European capitals, often leaving turmoil in his wake. Its political, social and creative ideals were also

We will free Italy from her innumerable museums that cover her like countless cemeteries.
Manifesto of Futurism, 1909

disseminated in numerous manifestos on subjects as diverse as music and lust, thus employing industrial means of production and distribution to spread its message as widely as possible. In the *Manifesto of Futurist Painters*, written by Boccioni with Giacomo Balla, Carlo Carrà, Gina Severini and Luigi Russolo, the authors pronounced they would 'support and glory in our day-to-day world, a world that is going to be continually and splendidly transformed by victorious Science'.

Bringing art to life

Despite its celebration of the potentialities of mass production, Futurism struggled to make its engagement with the wider world more than symbolic. Its most famous architectural expression remained on paper, in a series of powerful sketches, *Città Nuova* (New City), exhibited by the young architect Antonio Sant'Elia in Milan, in 1914. These radical drawings depicted massive, stepped buildings – mass housing, power stations, transport interchanges – with service towers thrusting into the sky, connected by gantries, bridges and multilevel highways, all constructed of concrete and iron. Marinetti recruited Sant'Elia to the Futurist cause, despite the clash between these monumental structures and his own belief in a light, flexible architecture of change, in which 'our houses will last less time than we do'. Sant'Elia's exhibition statement was published as *Futurist Architecture: A Manifesto*, declaring that 'the decorative must be abolished' and calling for the city to be rebuilt 'like an immense and tumultuous shipyard, active, mobile, and everywhere dynamic'. His death during World War I ensured his industrialized visions would never be realized, yet they remain eerily prescient of international architectural movements that flourished half a century later.

A few Futurists, such as Balla and scenographer Enrico Prampolini, made smaller-scale forays into design, for instance in the geometric murals and furniture in Balla's own homes in Düsseldorf and Rome. And Balla found an unexpectedly productive outlet in fashion, rejecting conventional clothes as 'tight-fitting, colourless, funereal, decadent, boring and unhygienic' and proposing ever-changing Futurist suits – aggressive, colourful, asymmetrical, phosphorescent 'clothing machines' with light bulbs and pneumatic systems – so 'everyone can alter his dress according to the needs of his spirit'.

But Futurism's furthest-reaching impact came in typography. Seeking to explode the staid rigidity of the book, Marinetti's poetry employed unfettered layouts to convey both the meaning and sounds of his words, mixing typefaces across the page, slanting text in different directions, adding rules, arrows and mathematical symbols, while eschewing both syntax and punctuation. Early examples employed traditional letterpress, but Marinetti and his fellow Futurists also exploited the greater freedom of photographic collages, adding handwritten text, imagery, or even fragments of advertising, to increase visual impact. This total poetry of *parole in libertà* – words in freedom – allowed the intensity of cities, emotions and wars to be communicated, and briefly found a wider outlet in the radical Florentine literary journal *Lacerba*. Subsequent Modernist movements, from Dada to Constructivism, made heavy use of these newfound typographical freedoms, and they soon entered mainstream publishing and advertising.

A troubled decline

Futurism's international influence was indisputable. In Japan and Brazil, for instance, it achieved an immediate sensation, aided by translations of Marinetti's manifesto appearing in newspapers (*Subaru* and *Jornal de Notícias* respectively) within months. Yet many international groupings with an ostensible affinity chose to emphasize their distance from the controversial movement – for example, Britain's Vorticists and the Russian Futurists, both of whom carved their own distinctive paths after early contact with the Italians.

In common with other movements of the era, the arrival of war seriously curtailed the Futurists' progress, as its leading lights volunteered to serve. In 1916, Boccioni died, falling from a horse during a training exercise. Afterwards, Futurism began to fade, its reputation already sullied by the group's virulent anti-Austrian pronouncements, and further harmed by Marinetti's post-war support of Benito Mussolini's Fascists, an association from which the movement never recovered. In addition, the realities of a destructive, modern, technology-driven conflict ensured that Futurism's earlier exaltation of the machine no longer seemed so exhilarating. The result was a move back towards more traditional approaches to art in Italy, a trend characterized as the 'return to order'.

Despite this waning, the Futurist aesthetic remained potent, deployed in the determinedly apolitical world of Art Deco, from glassware and ceramics to fabrics and advertising. In particular, Fortunato Depero, author with Balla of *Futurist Reconstruction of the Universe*, created highly successful, striking, black-and-white adverts for Campari in the 1920s, as well as his famous conical bottle for Campari Soda, re-employing Futurist techniques to commercial ends. Depero claimed the movement's influence was everywhere, saying, 'I see it on every street corner, on every space reserved for advertising, more or less plagiarized or stolen, with more or less intelligence, more or less taste. . .I am delighted.' His career took him to New York, and to *Vanity Fair* and *Vogue*, further proof of Futurism's visual punch, as well as its intellectual freedom, both qualities embraced with vigour by the high-tech and Postmodernist movements in the 1980s.

The condensed idea
Rejecting the past, transforming the future

14 Constructivism

Constructivism emerged in Russia following the Bolshevik Revolution of 1917. In this brave new world, the time was ripe for a movement that aspired to take the visual arts in an entirely new direction. It reimagined artistic production as an activity at the disposal of a greater social project, reawakening the consciousness of the masses and pushing forward the revolutionary agenda. The Constructivist was less a traditional artist pursuing self-expression, more a technician or engineer cerebrally 'constructing' their work. There was a firm focus on the principles of industrial production, with preferred materials being glass, metal and wood. The visual language was stripped back, too, with ornamentation exchanged for abstract, geometric forms. It was a creed that, during the movement's brief life span, informed important aspects of the Soviet Union's design environment, from where it exerted international influence.

Artistic roots

Constructivism drew heavily on European avant-garde abstraction, including Cubism and Futurism. One of its founding fathers, Vladimir Tatlin, had been enormously influenced by a visit to Picasso's Paris studio in 1913. Spellbound by a series of wooden reliefs, he created his own abstract pieces from industrial materials, somewhere between sculpture and design, that he called 'Corner Counter Reliefs'. Exhibited in St Petersburg in 1915, they offered a blueprint for the Constructivists to come. Meanwhile, Kazimir Malevich was evolving his philosophy of Suprematism, rejecting the notion that art ought somehow to copy nature, instead elucidating an abstract art that was produced systematically, almost mathematically, to convey a sense of dynamism, technology and social upheaval. Suprematism established much of the visual language adopted by Constructivists, but these evocations of pure feeling were out of kilter with their utilitarian ambitions.

Making a statement

The first use of the term 'constructivism' was by the sculptor Naum Gabo in the 1920 *Realistic Manifesto*, which rejected artistic conventions for an art grounded in material realities. The movement was refined during a series of debates over the following two years at Moscow's Institute of Artistic Culture (INKhUK), its war cry appearing in Aleksei Gan's manifesto for the group: 'We declare uncompromising war on art'. By then, Tatlin had designed its enduring icon, the unbuilt Monument to the Third International, intended as the headquarters for the recently founded Comintern (an organization to promote communism globally). It was to have been built from glass and steel, dwarfing the Eiffel Tower at 400m (1,310ft) tall, with its four revolving glass volumes housing the legislature, government offices, a press office and, at the top, a radio station with equipment to project slogans into the clouds.

Constructivism announced itself on the world stage at the 1925 Exposition internationale in Paris with Konstantin Melnikov's angular Soviet Pavilion. Rejecting the fair's Art Deco frivolity, it housed a collection of everyday industrial goods, plus a workers' reading room designed by Alexander Rodchenko – one of the few fully realized pieces of Constructivist design. Prioritizing community and frugality in contrast to the fair's prevailing luxury, the room was made from cheap standardized wooden parts, with space-saving multifunctional furniture, from a swivelling chessboard to an expandable 'living newspaper' unit, with slide-projection screen, poster wall, podium and rostrum all crammed in. It reflected Constructivist ambitions to design standardized, flexible, mass-produced furnishings for workers' apartments in Soviet Russia, helping them eat, sleep and live in one compact space. Severe in appearance, such designs found meaning in the expression of their construction and function.

Harsh realities

Despite a wealth of inventive designs, economic and cultural factors were not kind to Constructivism. All proposals had to match the availability of materials and manufacturing across the Soviet Union's strictly planned economy. Ageing factories were widely scattered around the country, and resources to tool up for new designs were lacking. Even rare official commissions tended to remain on paper, while 'design', with its capitalist overtones, was a forbidden word. Increasingly, Rodchenko advocated 'productivism', abandoning the ambition to integrate art and society in favour of a direct engagement with the means of production and the needs of society.

Among the most influential teachers of 'Art in Production' was El Lissitzky, whose influential painting *Beat the Whites with the Red Wedge* (1919) used abstraction to political ends, depicting the Red Army of the Bolsheviks as a red triangle penetrating the white circle of the anti-communist White Army. Less severe than Rodchenko, El Lissitzky taught his students to design multifunctional systems, including everything from built-in furniture to pots and pans, tailored precisely to the specific layouts of each apartment block. He informed his students that furnishings should be geometric, industrial and simple 'not from any paucity of artistic energy or inventive fantasy, but from a richness that tends towards the laconic – they are primal.' Through its functional exactitude, Constructivist furniture aimed to do more than meet users' needs; it determined how they were to live in the new socialist state. Despite educational pushes and instruction manuals, however, few took up the challenge – or even, with so few designs in production, had the opportunity.

Fashion flair

Varvara Stepanova – one of the two most successful women in the movement alongside Lyubov Popova – was most renowned for her forays into textile and clothes design. With Soviet Russia cut off from Europe's fashion capitals, Stepanova and Popova between them produced hundreds of designs for the First State Textile Factory, as well as teaching textile design. Drawing on traditional peasant garments and abstract trends, Stepanova created clothes that used angular forms to accentuate the sense of the human body in action. Among her most successful garments were unisex jumpsuits that found use in factories, sporting arenas and homes. In terms of seeing her art translated into mass-produced, mass-circulated utilitarian objects, she was arguably the most successful Constructivist of them all.

Transmitting messages

Propaganda proved a more fruitful outlet for Constructivist artists, with Alexander Rodchenko arguably the most gifted graphic designer. Most famous of his works is the 1924 poster, *Books (Please)! In All Branches of Knowledge*, with its photomontage of an ebullient woman worker exclaiming the titular demand – a genre-defining piece that continues to inspire imitations even now. Such bold combinations of geometric forms, photographic collage, strong colours and striking typography briefly became a staple of the Soviet Union's visual lingua franca, and the movement's artists became associated with agitprop, a phrase derived from the Department of Agitation and Propaganda, which used culture to spread the revolutionary message. To reach a largely rural, semi-literate population, agit-trains were introduced, which toured the country showing news reels and disseminating propaganda. The trains themselves bore artworks by leading Constructivists including El Lissitzky and Vladimir Mayakovsky.

Endings

For all its apparent symmetry with the ruling regime, the movement nonetheless fell from favour, accused of a utopian detachment from everyday life and excessive formalism; the INKhUK closed down in 1930. Fearing Constructivism's avant-garde nature and intellectualism, Stalin instead supported Neoclassical architecture and Socialist Realist art, with its idealized images of heroic factory workers and farmers. However, Constructivism's international influence endured and, through the Bauhaus and De Stijl, provided the moral and intellectual basis that underpinned Modernism in the decades to come.

The condensed idea
New design for a new society

15 De Stijl

The most significant new Dutch school to emerge in the aftermath of World War I was De Stijl, which translates as 'The Style'. Led by Theo van Doesburg and, most famously, Piet Mondrian, it championed a stark new visual language based on an idealistic faith in the transformative qualities of art. Seeking to provide insight into the laws governing the harmony of the world, it championed an abstract style based on strict but simple geometric forms and primary colours. Although relatively short-lived, its influence was significant across art, architecture and design.

Neoplasticism

De Stijl announced itself to the world in 1917, in the form of a magazine of the same name, which served as a vehicle for the ideas of its two main protagonists. In articles spread over several issues, the pair explored their philosophy of art, with Mondrian coining the term *de nieuwe beelding* (neoplasticism; or 'the new plastic art') to describe it. They demanded the abandonment of any semblance of naturalistic representation in favour of what became the group's signature straight lines, rectangles and basic colour palette – all in the search for an order and balance that seemed in short supply in the world.

Their influences were myriad, including the Cubists, Dadaists and Suprematists, along with a relatively obscure treatise published in 1916, 'The Principles of Plastic Mathematics' by the academic M H J Schoenmaekers. This argued that reality consists of opposing forces, such as the horizontal and the vertical, and the primary colours. In Mondrian's own words:

> 'As a pure representation of the human mind, art will express itself in an aesthetically purified, that is to say, abstract form. The new plastic idea cannot, therefore, take the form of a natural or concrete representation – this new plastic idea will ignore the particulars of appearance, that is to say, natural form and colour. On the contrary it should find its expression in the abstraction of form and colour, that is to say, in the straight line and the clearly defined primary colour.'

The movement became synonymous with Mondrian's geometric abstractions – rectilinear forms in red, blue, yellow, white and black filling canvases and becoming almost a short-hand for 'modern art' in its entirety in the popular imagination.

The search for harmony

Among De Stijl's circle were the artists Vantongerloo, Bart van der Leck and Vordemberge-Gildewart, along with the architects J J P Oud and Gerrit Rietveld, all looking to bring together the fine arts with architecture, industrial design and typography. Despite the apparent austerity of its style, the movement was significantly successful in doing so, not least in its lasting influence over Modernist designers and architects during the 1920s and beyond.

Rietveld – the son of a cabinet maker – was responsible for a series of speculative furniture designs, including one of the group's canonical works, the Red and Blue Chair. Using rectilinear wooden panels and struts – plain when first designed in 1918, painted in the group's accepted palette to accentuate the structure in 1923 – the result was wholly unnaturalistic, with the two elements of the seat seeming to float in space, yet still appeared entirely balanced. Moreover, Rietveld crafted the piece from standard-sized lumber, with a view to it being capable of mass production. He was also responsible for another important staging post in the group's evolution, the Rietveld Schröder House (see box), for which he later designed his much-copied cantilevered Zig-Zag chair. Its daring, Z-shaped form – originally constructed from four cupboard shelves, but intended to be made from a single piece of wood – was a tribute to Theo van Doesburg, and his contentious and divisive embrace of the diagonal.

The split

During time spent in Weimar in the early 1920s, van Doesburg failed to inveigle himself onto the faculty of the Bauhaus, but did succeed in introducing a new focus on rationality and uniformity to the school, helping sweep aside its expressive tendencies. While there, he also organized an ambitious Congress of Constructivists and Dadaists in 1922, attended by leading Constructivist El Lissitzky and future Bauhaus professor László Moholy-Nagy, among many other Modernist luminaries. Moving to Paris, he then undertook a series of works entitled 'Counter Compositions' (1924–25) that marked his adoption of a new theory of art that he called Elementarism, shifting from the sole utilization of horizontals and verticals towards the prioritization of the diagonal, with lines emerging at 45 degrees from the picture frame. Elementarism, he declared, was 'based on the neutralization of positive and negative directions by the diagonal and, as far as colour is concerned, by the dissonant'. To Mondrian,

Rietveld Schröder House

Built in 1924, in the Dutch city of Utrecht, for the recently widowed Truus Schröder-Schräder, the Rietveld Schröder House is regarded as the only complete De Stijl building in existence. Not wishing to be constrained by tradition, Schröder-Schräder collaborated with Gerrit Rietveld to create a home that provided simplicity and space, and the opportunity for her and her children to live as they pleased. The result is an asymmetrical yet balanced composition of intersecting slabs, posts and beams, enhanced by the characteristic De Stijl colour scheme. Transitions between exterior and interior are frictionless, while sliding walls inside allow great spatial flexibility. The extensive use of ingenious built-in furniture turns the entire house into a complex yet fully resolved piece of cabinetry – a 'total work of art'.

this was anathema – van Doesburg's colour palette had even grown to include grey.

> We speak of concrete and not abstract, because nothing is more concrete, more real than a line, a colour, a surface.
>
> Theo van Doesburg, 1930

The De Stijl rules left little room for manoeuvre, and now van Doesburg was casting their tenets on the purity of line and colour into doubt. Unable to find a compromise, Mondrian left the group. Van Doesburg duly set out his new philosophy in a manifesto in which he defended the modification of the group's ethos, suggesting that it had been dogmatic and that the diagonal provided for greater dynamism in their work. When van Doesburg died in 1931, the movement found itself without a leader and quickly dissolved. Yet its influence was persistent, with its pared-back, abstract approach informing designers and architects across the decades. In 1965, the fashion designer Yves Saint Laurent released his Mondrian Collection, based on the Dutchman's artworks. By then, the artist had been dead more than 20 years, but the collection won great acclaim and became an iconic milestone in Saint Laurent's career. That Mondrian's vision was capable of enchanting the fashion set some half a century after he unleashed it onto the world proved the power of the group's legacy.

The condensed idea
The harmony of line and colour

16 The Bauhaus

Despite ceaseless efforts by design historians to propose alternatives, all roads in modern design still lead to and from the Bauhaus. Some have since ranged far, but the fundamental belief in design's power to chart a progressive future draws on this one, short-lived art school. During its 1920s peak, the Bauhaus aspired to harness mass production to improve lives and express modernity. By uniting the arts and engaging with new technologies, it sought to create standardized products that would be universal in aesthetics, functionality and affordability. During the Bauhaus's brief life, and in large part due to its impact, industrial design shifted from a tentative, ill-defined concept into concrete reality.

From craft to industry

Founded in 1919 in the small German city of Weimar by architect Walter Gropius, the Bauhaus – a newly coined term meaning 'house of building' – offered a comprehensive design education under the banner 'Art and Craft: A New Unity'. A knowledge of craft was deemed vital to the creative imagination, while artistic expression was given precedence over industry, in part due to lingering suspicion of the latter's role in World War I. A pioneering six-month 'preliminary course', developed by the mystically inclined Swiss artist Johannes Itten, and led by visual artists such as Paul Klee and Wassily Kandinsky, immersed students in materials, nature, composition, colour and form. Undertaken with almost spiritual intensity, these studies were intended, in Itten's words, 'to liberate the creative forces and thereby the artistic talents of the students', helping them choose which of the Bauhaus's workshops – metal, cabinetry, pottery, glass, wall-painting, weaving and more – to join. Despite Gropius's declarations of inclusivity, female students, initially in the majority, were pushed towards weaving and ceramics, reflecting his desire to portray an image of seriousness to state authorities funding the school, but also his chauvinism about women's creative abilities.

In 1923, Gropius bowed to pressure from those authorities, sceptical of the Bauhaus's politics and products, and also from peers, who complained that the school's failure to design for mass production

Standardized luxury

Many iconic products emerged from the Bauhaus, but Marcel Breuer's Wassily Chair – designed in 1925 in tribute to the classic club armchair and named after fellow teacher Wassily Kandinsky – tops the pile. The typology's traditional hefty slabs are replaced by a lightweight structure of tubular steel inspired by bicycle frames, across which thin straps of fabric are stretched, creating a geometric sculpture composed of empty space 'as if sketched into the room', as Breuer put it. Such designs were 'constructed from the same standardized, elementary parts that can be disassembled and interchanged at any time', yet these industrial ambitions did not match the handcrafted reality. Costly materials and cutting-edge aesthetics ensured that the Wassily Chair remained in production only briefly, finally reaching wider audiences after its equally pricey 1960s reissue. When first unveiled, the Wassily Chair seemed revolutionary in both concept and appearance, encapsulating the machine age, modern living and universality. Despite its familiarity, it still feels radical today.

undermined its commitment to social change. 'Technology' was substituted for 'craft' in its main slogan, and an additional one introduced, 'Art into Industry', while Itten was replaced by Hungarian painter and photographer László Moholy-Nagy, who believed that industrial materials and technology could unlock both artistic and social progress. Increasingly, a vocabulary of abstract geometric forms – cones, spheres, cubes, cylinders – was used to create prototypical objects with strikingly modern appearances, from Wilhelm Wagenfeld's hemispherical table lamp to Marianne Brandt's equally hemispherical teapot, but their practicality and suitability for mass production varied widely. Attempts were made to expand relationships with local industry, including factory visits and advisory services, with limited success.

A factory of design

In 1925, the Bauhaus moved to the more welcoming environment of Dessau, a rising town that hoped to harness this famed design school to boost its industry. At the new site, Gropius oversaw the construction of an extraordinary complex of spacious Modernist buildings in steel, concrete and glass, including his own eye-catching Bauhaus building with state-of-the-art workshops, studios, accommodation, offices and an auditorium. By now, the faculty comprised some of the most influential names in 20th-century design, including Herbert Bayer, Marianne Brandt, Anni and Josef Albers, Oskar Schlemmer, Marcel Breuer and Gunta Stölzl, and an architecture department was finally created under Swiss architect Hannes Meyer. Assisted by its own generous flow of promotional books, magazines and exhibitions, the Bauhaus was now acknowledged as the premier design institution of the age, even if the contribution of its handcrafted products to industrial and social change remained mostly symbolic.

Broken apart

Gropius left the Bauhaus in 1928 to concentrate on his architectural practice, but his successor Hannes Meyer – a 'scientific Marxist' who believed in 'the needs of the people, not the needs of luxury' – somewhat surprisingly forged more lucrative relationships with industry. Lighting, textiles and, in particular, a range of severe wallpapers proved highly successful, but the fractious and dogmatic

Meyer was dismissed for his political activities in 1930, by which time such major figures as Moholy-Nagy, Breuer and Bayer had departed. Under the new director, Ludwig Mies van der Rohe, the school was increasingly embattled, attracting growing antagonism from right-wing officials for its progressive and internationalist ethos, as well as its avant-garde aesthetics. Despite a further reorientation

Every age demands its own form. It is our task to design the new world with existing tools.
Hannes Meyer, 1926

towards architecture, the city council in Dessau voted for its closure in 1932. The Bauhaus relocated to Berlin to attempt to survive as a private institution, making a few unfortunate political compromises along the way, but accepted the inevitable the following year, closing itself in the face of persecution by the new Nazi government.

Scattered across the world by the hostile climate of 1930s Germany, Bauhaus teachers and students ensured that its products, curriculum and principles became foundational pillars for Modernist design. Attempting to summarize the Bauhaus – its activities, ambitions and achievements, its personal and professional rivalries, the extravagant praise and censure it has attracted over the years, its capacity for experimentation and joy, captured in black-and-white photos of students on staircases and stages – is largely futile. Reading about the school in greater depth, however, is hugely rewarding.

The condensed idea
Art and technology: a new unity

17 Surrealism

Rising to prominence in the 1920s, Surrealism represented a rejection of the so-called rationalism of European culture in favour of giving expression to the unconscious mind in pursuit of a super-reality (or surreality). The resulting works were dreamlike, counterintuitive and disconcerting, full of surprising imagery, non sequiturs and juxtapositions. Political as well as artistic, the movement aimed at liberating the individual by finding wonder in the strange and unconventional, and challenging and transgressing accepted norms. From its roots as a countercultural movement, Surrealism came to wield enormous and enduring cultural influence.

Breton's manifesto

The beginnings of the Surrealist movement date back to 1924, when the French writer André Breton published his *Surrealist Manifesto*, taking inspiration from a radical tradition that included Karl Marx and the 19th-century transgressive French poet, Arthur Rimbaud, as well as the reason-defying Dadaists and the earlier realism-rejecting Symbolists. Breton defined Surrealism as 'psychic automatism', in which the expression of thought through the act of creation is dictated by the thought itself, unmitigated by the exercise of reason or any aesthetic or moral concern. It was a philosophy that chimed with the work of the Austrian neurologist, Sigmund Freud, whose investigations into the subconscious fascinated Surrealist artists. During the mid-1920s, the movement began its transition into the cultural mainstream, with practitioners increasingly working in commercial fields, from advertising and graphic design to film and theatre.

Crossing into the commercial

The leading Surrealist artists became household names – figures like Joan Miró, René Magritte and, above all, Salvador Dalí. Works such as Magritte's *The Son of Man* (featuring a man in a bowler hat, his face obscured by a hovering green apple) and Dalí's *The Persistence of Memory* (with its melting clocks) transcended the world of fine art to become serially reproduced and adapted icons of popular culture. Surrealism's popular success, combined with the considerable intellectual and personal ambitions of its leaders, ensured that the movement became increasingly engaged with the material world.

Initially, this took the form of sculptures that adopted familiar forms or utilizing found objects, many of them commercial, and thus already rich in meaning. Through free association and unexpected juxtapositions, combined with overt eroticism and a wry humour, such sculptural objects explored the strangeness of modern life, while also critiquing society's fetishism of commodities. Dalí was, as ever, at the forefront of developments, citing Michelangelo's costumes for the Vatican's Swiss Guard when proclaiming that 'the modern artist should participate in every kind of extracurricular activity'. His 1936 *Lobster Telephone*, created for the home of the wealthy poet Edward James, is the single most recognizable Surrealist object, the unlikely juxtaposition impelling reconsideration of two individually familiar objects, of which Dalí said, 'I do not understand why, when I ask for a grilled lobster in a restaurant, I am never served cooked telephone.'

> I try to create fantastic things, magical things, like in a dream. The world needs more fantasy.
>
> Salvador Dalí, 1940

Subverting the everyday

But the story by no means began and ended with Dalí. Méret Oppenheim, for instance, achieved notoriety with works such as her fetishistic gazelle-fur-covered cup and saucer, created in 1936 as a riposte to a comment from Picasso on her fur-clad bracelet. Similarly, Óscar Domínguez created plush upholstery for a wooden wheelbarrow, carrying a hint of the bordello. Utilized as a fashion prop by photographer Man Ray – an early example of the embrace of Surrealist imagery by the world of couture – Domínguez's *Brouette* presaged a world of 'design art', eliding the distinctions between the two disciplines and opening collectors' wallets.

Some adapted Surrealist attitudes to more practical ends, for instance architect and designer Carlo Mollino, who incorporated cast-plaster body fragments into his interiors and employed a rich visual language rooted in organic forms for his furnishings, epitomized by the sensual shapes of his tables. Known as biomorphism, this free-form approach was adopted by designers as diverse as Isamu Noguchi

Domestic Surrealism

Home, in Freudian dream analysis, is where our emotional and psychological lives are at their most intense, packed with symbolic spaces, from staircases to doorways, and providing a rich source of raw material for the Surrealist. In this vein, the wealthy collector Edward James – described by Salvador Dalí as a 'humming-bird poet' – concocted theatrical Surrealist interiors for his London and West Sussex homes. His commissions ranged from a staircase carpet woven with the imprints of wet feet to a tea service decorated with intertwining pink gloves. Most famous are the works James created with Dalí, including several versions of the *Lobster Telephone*, floor lamps constructed of oversized champagne glasses, and two bright-red Mae West Lips sofas for his Sussex dining room.

James deliberately cherished a childlike approach to both life and art, rejecting traditional expectations around domesticity. Later he decamped to the remote village of Xilitla in Mexico, calling the country 'the Surrealist place par excellence'. There, in the midst of the rainforest, he created another Surrealist dreamworld, Las Pozas, complete with a fantastical series of massive concrete sculptures in vibrant colours that remained unfinished on his death.

and Gaetano Pesce to very different, but highly effective ends. Advertising and graphic design also proved fertile ground for Surrealist artists, with Dalí, Magritte and Man Ray all accepting commissions. Having moved to Britain in 1932, German artist Hans Schleger included Surrealist imagery in his work for major corporations, including London Transport and Shell, under the name Zero, for instance taking inspiration from Magritte's *Le Faux Miroir* (with clouds floating within a large, open eye) to inform one celebrated poster for the 'You Can Be Sure of Shell' series.

The marriage of fashion design and Surrealism was perhaps inevitable, given the movement's fascination with desire and the symbolism of the body – particularly the female body and its constituent parts. Photographers such as Man Ray and Horst P Horst were conspicuously successful, as was Italian designer Elsa Schiaparelli, collaborating with Surrealist artists, including Dalí, Oppenheim and Aragon, while dressing Marlene Dietrich, Katharine Hepburn, Greta Garbo and Lauren Bacall among others. Her eye-catching creations included her provocative Shoe Hat, featuring an upturned pink velvet high heel, and her elegant, yet uncanny, Skeleton Dress, with its prominent quilted 'bones'. Such designs were show-stopping and subversive but also, crucially, wearable, engendering a Surrealist vogue within fashion that was much employed both in shop windows and cultural bibles *Harper's* and *Vogue*, achieving a cultural crossover that remains in place even today.

Staying power

The Surrealist movement lost momentum and fashionability with the onset of World War II, and the death of Breton in 1966 seemed to bring the curtain down once and for all. However, the powerful work of female Surrealists such as Mimi Parent, Leonora Carrington and Dorothea Tanning in the post-war period has recently received renewed attention, indicating that Surrealism's ability to challenge norms endured. Surrealism also received vocal acclaim from Postmodernists in the 1980s and fashion designers such as Alexander McQueen and Jean-Paul Gaultier in the 1990s, and its privileging of the unexpected, emphasis on free-form expression and self-exploration, and sheer variety of form continue to be a potent combination.

The condensed idea
Expressing our unconscious desires

18 The Paperback

It is rare that a design innovation to an established product makes truly meaningful ripples in the world. Of relatively recent vintage, one might cite the iPhone as not merely shaking up the mobile phone business, but fundamentally altering our relationship with communications technology. But when the publisher, Allen Lane, unleashed the potential of the paperback in the 1930s, he was revolutionizing a format – the bound book – that had been around for 2,000 years. His perspicacity would reshape the publishing industry, and alter the reading habits of millions, perhaps even billions. And legend suggests it all came about as he waited for a train at an English West Country railway station.

Quality for all

The story goes that, in 1934, Lane, chairman of the esteemed Bodley Head publishing house, was returning from a literary weekend in Devon with crime author Agatha Christie. These were bleak economic times, and he worried for the company's future as he waited at Exeter station for his train back to London. Forever monitoring the market, he scanned the platform bookstall, and found himself appalled at the trash on offer. What, he wondered, if he could work out how to make good-quality reprints of worthwhile literature available for a reasonable price – equivalent to, say, a packet of ten cigarettes?

From this kernel of an idea, a mighty publishing oak sprang. With Bodley Head initially unwilling to back his idea, he raised the capital himself, and set up a new imprint – Penguin – with his brothers, Richard and John. Getting started was tough. Publishers were reluctant to grant reprint rights, unsure what this imprudent venture might mean for their futures, while bookshops refused to make the advance orders needed for viability – a last-minute sale of 63,500 copies to Woolworths proved crucial. The first ten titles – a mix of fiction and non-fiction, including works by Agatha Christie, Ernest

> We believed in the existence in this country of a vast reading public for intelligent books at a low price, and staked everything on it.
>
> Allen Lane

Hemingway and Dorothy L Sayers – hit the shops on 30 July 1935. All 20,000 copies of each sold out immediately. Within six months, Penguin had its first million sales, and accelerated from there.

Yet the paperback – that is to say, a softcover book typically stuck with glue rather than stitched or stapled – was not a new invention. Nor was Lane's sprinkling of quality into the mix – German publisher Tauchnitz had been reprinting revered English-language authors in paperback since 1841. Yet the vast majority of paperbacks dealt in pulp fiction, while also covering their readers' hands in ink. In contrast to American 'dime novels' or British 'yellowbacks', Lane's genius was to fill his books with brilliant words and package them as truly desirable objects.

A design classic

Improved technology made it possible for Penguin to use cleaner ink on better paper, but its mastery of graphic design and brand identity was crucial. Where most publishers distinguished covers by emphasizing the book's title and author, Penguin's books – all of uniform size, and initially clad in a dust jacket – sported simple geometric covers devoid of gaudy visuals, with their bold horizontal stripes highlighting the brand above all. Title and author were printed in the classic Gill Sans font, with books colour-coded by genre, including orange for fiction, green for crime and blue for biography. Then, of course, there was the beguiling logo on every cover. Even as rivals launched, Penguin paperbacks shone from book racks as beacons of style and culture, garnering sales to match.

A blueprint for others

In 1936, having gained its independence, Penguin launched a new imprint, Pelican. Dedicated to 'intellectual' non-fiction, it opened with a reprint of George Bernard Shaw's *The Intelligent Woman's Guide to Socialism, Capitalism and Sovietism*. When approached, Shaw jumped at the opportunity, saying that 'a sixpenny edition would be the salvation of mankind', adding 'fascism' to its title and penning extra content. The following year, the journalistic Penguin Specials arrived, in which leading authors tackled subjects of international concern – the first, *Germany Puts the Clock Back* by Edgar Mowrer, sold 50,000 copies in a week. When it came, World War II proved a

A raft of penguins

Penguin's name is supposed to have been suggested by Lane's secretary, Joan Coles, inspired by Albatross Books, a German paperback imprint founded in 1932 but curtailed by war – also colour-coded, also printing Agatha Christie, and also sporting an eye-catching bird logo. A 21-year-old designer, Edward Young, was promptly sent to London Zoo to sketch one of the said birds – a task he completed despite complaining of the stink. There have been several redesigns since – it even danced for a while in the 1930s – with Jan Tschichold crafting its current form in 1946, followed by a slight slimming in 2003 for better rendering on thin spines. Nonetheless, the company insignia remains clearly descended from Young's original, and Lane was sufficiently satisfied to entrust him with the design of the Pelican logo too.

boom time for the company, with its lightweight product popular with troops abroad and evacuated children – although the new Puffin books for the young struggled to source rationed paper. Penguin Modern Painters suffered no such problems, as it fell into the category of propaganda, while the Handbooks series tackled pertinent wartime subjects such as growing soft fruit and rabbit farming. After the Labour Party's landslide victory at the 1945 general election, its leader Clement Attlee commented: 'After the WEA [Workers' Educational Association], it was Lane and his Penguins that did most to get us into office at the end of the war.'

Noting Penguin's success, Pocket Books introduced a similar model in the United States in 1939 – although with a less distinctive design – distributing their paperbacks alongside magazines to ensure their ubiquity. During the war, the US military sent over 120 million special-edition paperbacks from Pocket Books and rapidly established rivals to its troops for free. France had to wait until 1953 for its equivalent, *Le Livre de Poche* (The Pocket Book), but there was no doubting that Lane had ignited the paperback's international blossoming – the format was here to stay.

Changing times, stylish designs

To Lane's regret, as competition grew, selling Penguins on the power of the brand proved less fruitful. To cut through on shelves, each cover needed to be treated individually, and with more edge. But, as a believer that 'good design is no more expensive than bad', Lane made sure to employ the best. The renowned German typographer Jan Tschichold evolved a sophisticated design strategy in the post-war years, devising strict rules to be applied across all series, and designing elegant covers for the Penguin Classics and Shakespeare series. Others with impeccable Modernist credentials followed, including another German, Hans Schmoller, the Italian Germano Facetti and the Polish Romek Marber, whose 'Marber Grid' set the template for future generations of Penguin titles, providing an adaptable, updated yet unmistakable company look.

Lane had delivered a format so simple and successful that, again to his annoyance, the words Penguin and paperback became synonymous. Yet his idea was not the paperback, it was the quality paperback. He sought to make first-class content available to all, and package it in the best possible fashion. It was a perfect design, one that has outlasted repeated predictions of its demise, and is set fair to fill shelves for generations to come.

The condensed idea
The unimprovable format

19 Organic Design

Not everyone warmed to the chrome-plated furniture of 1920s and 1930s Modernism. It was glamorous, sculptural, cleanable, but not necessarily liveable, and definitely not cheap. As early as 1931, Maurice Dufrène of Paris's leading department store, Galeries Lafayette, attacked tubular-steel chairs as neutral, anonymous and mechanical – 'the root cause of the great Dullness'. Modernist furnishings came in for a particularly hard time in Sweden and Britain, depicted as flashy and ridiculous, especially in domestic contexts, and derided by author Aldous Huxley: 'To dine off an operating table, to loll in a dentist's chair – this is not my idea of domestic bliss.'

New possibilities

For avant-garde consumers looking for something a little less clinical, an alternative was on the horizon. In 1930, the Stockholm Exhibition introduced a gentler Modernism, with bright, airy pavilions set amid relaxed, colourful surroundings, displaying well-made, well-designed 'everyday objects'. Head architect Gunnar Asplund stated his desire to create something quite different from the severity of equivalent German events, instead 'fulfilling the requirements of beauty and festivity'. This shift in emphasis pointed a way forward for many visitors, including the Finnish Modernist architect Alvar Aalto, who welcomed Stockholm's 'composition in houses, flags, searchlights, flowers, fireworks, happy people and clean tablecloths'.

Humanizing design

Since the late 1920s, Aalto had been looking to learn 'the language of wood fibres', hoping to adapt a cheap, plentiful material – Finnish birch – to Modernist goals of standardization and functionality. His experiments were due, in part, to expedience, but also to his growing belief that 'objects that can with justification be called "rational" often suffer from a considerable lack of human quality', with steel and chrome singled out for particular criticism. Tasked with designing a sanatorium at Paimio in southwest Finland in 1929, he and his wife Aino Marsio produced two groundbreaking armchairs. For one, a quintessential Modernist form – the bent-metal cantilevered chair –

was translated into wood. For the other, a curled plywood seat, angled to aid patients' breathing, was suspended from a striking birch frame. Both grabbed the attention of the design world, launching a design ethos sometimes termed 'humanist', sometimes 'biomorphic', but perhaps best described as 'organic'.

Aalto's innovations caught the eye of British critic Philip Morton Shand, who had also admired the 1930 Stockholm Exhibition, welcoming its 'wholesome Nordic sanity'. He sensed an opportunity to sell Aalto's furniture to progressive British consumers, betting on its domestic appeal and its relative affordability, throwing together an exhibition in fashionable London department store Fortnum & Mason in 1933, then setting up an import business, Finmar. Two years later, buoyed by its success, the Aaltos founded Artek (a composite of 'art' and 'technology') to promote and sell their furniture to the world, and the firm still exists today.

> **Form must have a content, and that content must be linked with nature.**
> Alvar Aalto, 1928

Jumping on bandwagons

In Britain, two companies had already been experimenting with plywood's potential for Modernist furniture, but encountering the Aaltos' products expanded their aesthetic, technical and commercial horizons. One, Makers of Simple Furniture, is famous for the first chair made from a single sheet of plywood, designed by the idiosyncratic founder Gerald Summers. This strikingly minimal object – and much of the firm's 'furniture for the concrete age' – was expensive and handcrafted, resulting in limited sales, despite backing from department stores in London and New York.

Isokon proved a more substantive rival, appointing the newly arrived Walter Gropius as controller of design after his escape from Germany in 1934, and then fellow refugee Marcel Breuer as head of design. Both Bauhaus heavyweights embraced plywood, with Breuer, the doyen of tubular steel, proving particularly successful. His supremely stylish Long Chair – a recliner with a moulded plywood seat and birch frame, based on an earlier aluminium design – was adopted as the company's logo. Once the pair left to the more enticing shores of the United States in 1937, Isokon appointed another émigré architect, Egon Riss, who strengthened plywood's relationship with middle-class intelligentsia by designing the iconic Penguin Donkey, a freestanding bookshelf specifically created to house paperbacks from the young publishing company. The coming of World War II brought production to an end, as plywood supplies dwindled.

Stool 60

Conceived in 1933 as cheap, stackable seating for a library they were designing in Vyborg, Stool 60 was among the first results of the Aaltos' experiments in bent wood, made in collaboration with manufacturer Otto Korhonen. The stool was stripped to its essentials: a circular birch seat covered in thin layers of plywood, with three birch legs curving 90 degrees at the top screwed to the underside. These 'L-legs' – 'the little sister of the architectural column', according to Aalto – solved the perennial design problem of attaching vertical legs to horizontal seats. Cutting thin slices into one end, then gluing strips of veneer into the cuts, allowed the wood to survive the bending process. As a result, the Modernist goal of a simple, standard component was realized in warm birch rather than hard metal, and eventually utilized on a range of more than 50 pieces. Production of Stool 60 has never ceased, making it one of the few design objects genuinely deserving of the designation 'timeless'.

Wider contexts

Although most countries proved less susceptible to plywood in the 1930s, Swedish designer Bruno Mathsson achieved a comparable humanism by experimenting with bent laminated beech. With its undulating frame and webbed seating, his innovative Eva Chair prioritized 'the mechanics of sitting' and, despite early misgivings at its startling appearance, remains in production today. Elsewhere, Modernist designers began, somewhat tentatively, to re-engage with historic furniture. Danish architect and educator Kaare Klint was the most influential, employing traditional forms and craftsmanship to achieve simple, elegant designs in solid wood that proved well suited to domestic interiors. Although the Aaltos' designs influenced the experimental moulded-plywood furniture created by Charles and Ray Eames from the 1940s, Klint's craft-oriented approach fostered a more conservative yet equally successful mid-century aesthetic, epitomized by two of Klint's talented pupils at the Danish Academy of Fine Arts, Hans Wegner and Børge Mogensen.

The condensed idea
Bringing together nature and Modernism

20 Planned Obsolescence

Planned obsolescence comes in many forms, but perhaps the earliest and most effective is fashion – rapid turns of style that make alluring objects outdated before they lose their usefulness. From the 1920s, the tactic was adopted by US automobile manufacturers seeking to absorb excess production capacity, who evolved it into something more comprehensive – and more sinister. The shift was spearheaded by the hugely successful, morally questionable, president of General Motors, Alfred P Sloan, who decreed that 'the laws of the Paris dressmakers have come to be a factor in the automobile industry – and woe to the company who ignores them'.

Mass-produced individuality

During its 17-year production run from 1908, more than 15 million Model T Fords were manufactured, making motoring increasingly affordable, but increasingly prosaic. And, with Ford's austere approach to specifications and colours, the Model T failed to offer the self-expression that consumers were finding in new Art Deco–influenced homewares. General Motors started the ball rolling on fashionable motoring by offering 24 colourful paint options for its Chevrolet Superior in 1924. Encouraging sales suggested that cosmetic tinkering might be more cost-effective in driving profit across the company's 'ladder of brands' – from mass-market Chevrolet to top-of-the-range Cadillac – than technological innovation.

In 1927, General Motors set up an 'Art and Color Section' under the young coachbuilder Harley Earl. Sloan's goal was to achieve 'continuous, eternal change', introducing new models every year but with only superficial upgrades, to 'create a certain amount of dissatisfaction with past models'. As a result, cars would be replaced before they lost their functionality, or their technology had been superseded. Earl's streamlined bodies also helped to disguise the messy assemblage of parts beneath, giving the illusion of technological progress while providing a canvas for an eye-catching array of bumpers, lights, trims and tailfins. To leverage the benefits of mass production, many parts were utilized across brands – even bodies from the 1930s – often trickling down from glamorous to cheaper models over successive years, thus encouraging people to remain on the ladder and aspire to a higher rung. Earl described his signature Cadillac tailfins as giving owners 'an extra receipt for the money in the form of a visible prestige marking for an expensive car'.

Within a few years, General Motors had achieved market leadership, and most car manufacturers were introducing their own styling departments, laying the ground for the famous chromed cars of the post-war era: 'jukeboxes on wheels, aesthetic aberrations that masked the workings of the machine beneath the layers of tawdry flash', in the disdainful opinion of Studebaker designer Raymond Loewy. Each brand reiterated its own twist on 'jet-age' style, with extravagant tailfins and bumpers, and an excess of headlights and portholes. From 1955, Virgil Exner's 'Forward Look' models for Chrysler introduced a sleek new take on the aesthetic, helping to usher Earl, and his bulkier designs, into retirement.

Pros and cons

Sloan's 'dynamic obsolescence' was soon adopted by other industries, and hailed by many as a force for good, stimulating demand, increasing productivity and driving employment, while giving consumers greater freedom of choice. Durable products, in contrast, were an economic drag, saturating and stifling markets. In a world of greater disposable income and ready credit, style was a route to sales success, dovetailing with growing sophistication in packaging and advertising.

Designer J Gordon Lippincott argued the case succinctly in 1947: 'Any method that can motivate the flow of merchandise to new buyers will create jobs and work for industry, and hence national prosperity. Our custom of trading in our automobiles every year, of having a new refrigerator, vacuum cleaner or

> Design these days means taking a bigger step every year. Our big job is to hasten obsolescence. In 1934 the average car ownership span was five years; now it is two years. When it is one year, we will have a perfect score.
> Harley Earl, 1955

electric iron every three or four years is economically sound. . .This is chiefly mental conditioning – largely a job of convincing the consumer that he needs a new product before his old one is worn out.'

The Phoebus cartel

In December 1924, representatives of the world's leading light bulb manufacturers, faced by increasing market volatility, gathered in Geneva to establish Phoebus SA, a cartel dividing the world into exclusive zones, and agreed to shorten the lifespan of bulbs from around 1,800 hours to a maximum of 1,000 hours. As the market and technology evolved, electric companies were no longer tasked with the maintenance of lighting systems, thus replacing bulbs had become the customer's responsibility – reducing their durability offered the tantalizing prospect of additional profit. Excessive energy consumption late in a bulb's lifespan was proffered as justification, but achieving the desired reduction in lifespans proved a significant engineering challenge (one that was never quite overcome) and required a testing laboratory in Switzerland to verify compliance – expenditures that could have been used to improve efficiency. The cartel fell apart with World War II, but the inefficient incandescent bulb survived for half a century until legislation intervened. Today, the market is once again shifting, with lighting companies once more installing and maintaining systems, making planned obsolescence of components a less enticing tactic.

Criticism gathered pace in the 1950s, when the term 'planned obsolescence' gained currency. It became clear that the tactic was not just about fashion – overly stylized products also reduced functionality, performance and repairability, offering further routes for companies to hasten the replacement of products, and the exploitation of consumers and resources. George Nelson, the doyen of the new breed of industrial designers, mounted a vigorous defence, stating that 'obsolescence as a process is wealth-producing, not hateful. . .What we need is more obsolescence, not less.' But *The Waste Makers* (1960) by journalist Vance Packard had greater impact, attacking manufacturers for pursuing strategies that ensured that 'wastefulness has become part of the American way of life', and creating a spiritually impoverished country burdened with debt and dissatisfaction. This chimed with growing ecological concerns, and distaste for corporate America's attitude towards its customers. Ralph Nader's 1965 *Unsafe at Any Speed*, the dramatic exposé of the automobile industry's disregard for safety (including its devotion to inherently dangerous tailfins), led to the imposition of mandatory standards by US Congress the following year.

There are qualities that are desperately needed for a sustainable model of manufacture – durability, repairability, recyclability, energy efficiency, responsibility and transparency. Yet more consumer goods are being produced than ever before, and the manufacturing and marketing of so many – smartphones, printer cartridges, clothes and cars – are still built upon transience, with sustainability treated as a sales tool rather than a philosophy. It seems that, as in the 1960s, it will take legislation to finally end planned obsolescence, and introduce a healthier relationship between products and the planet.

The condensed idea
The mass production of transience

21 Good Design

n the aftermath of World War II, there were some moves towards finding a more domestic, humane version of Modernism, but its essential premises remained largely unchallenged. A new crop of professional organizations emerged, along with a multitude of promotional exhibitions and publications, in which design was treated with a new seriousness as a form-making and problem-solving activity, and one with wide implications across industry and society. During the 1950s, the prevailing model of rational design, with a direct line back to the Bauhaus, appropriated the term 'good design' for itself, an association reinforced by a series of exhibitions of the same name at New York's Museum of Modern Art from 1950 until 1955. At the launch of the first of these, Dorothy Shaver, head of the Lord & Taylor department store, gave a concise summary of the movement: 'To me good design is simply art applied to living.'

Inheriting the mantle

Bolstered by European emigres, various US institutions in the pre-war years vied to be seen as the new centre of the Bauhaus tradition. Founded in 1933 in North Carolina, the experimental Black Mountain College flourished briefly under the aegis of Bauhaus alumni Josef and Anni Albers, producing a string of major talents such as Ruth Asawa, Robert Rauschenberg and Cy Twombly. In Chicago, the Hungarian-born László Moholy-Nagy was invited to set up a short-lived 'New Bauhaus' in 1937. The school stuck closely to its predecessor's avant-garde curriculum, with results that failed to match the commercial ambitions of its industrial backers. When absorbed into the Illinois Institute of Technology in 1949, however, it contributed to the genesis of America's leading design school, one largely shorn of the more expressive aspects of the Bauhaus, focusing instead on functionality and professionalization.

Forging a neo-functionalism

Over in Europe, there was only one true 'inheritor of the Bauhaus' – the Hochschule für Gestaltung (School of Design), founded in Ulm in 1953 and anointed by Walter Gropius as the 'new Bauhaus'. Its clean, sophisticated designs were crucial to fostering perceptions of West Germany as a leader in technology, industry and design. Although the first 'rector', the Bauhaus alumnus Max Bill, maintained an arts-inspired curriculum, internal tensions led to his departure. Afterwards, a more methodological, interdisciplinary approach was adopted, with the school's co-founder, graphic designer Otl Aicher, dismissing the original Bauhaus as having 'left more of a mark on the museum than on present-day technology and economy'.

Developing utilitarian, serviceable designs and building relationships with industry took precedence, but Bill's concept of *die gute Form* (usually translated as 'good design') remained a powerful influence, with its promotion of functional clarity as a source of both aesthetic and moral integrity. Commissions followed for a visual identity for Germany's national airline, Lufthansa, stretching from its tableware to its logo, and for Hamburg's transport system, from its signage to its colour schemes. The legacy of Ulm is most evident in products by the Braun electronics firm, which for a while existed in a symbiotic relationship with the institution. Having already imported two of the school's major figures, Otl Aicher and Hans Gugelot, in 1955 it recruited Dieter Rams, who although not an Ulm alumnus became a protégé of the other two.

> Good design is as little design as possible.
> Dieter Rams

As Braun's head of design from 1961, Rams ensured a consistent look across the firm's ranges – a clean, austere, striking aesthetic whether in a record player, shaver, desk fan or kitchen appliance. Each expressed its function through beautiful proportions – as in the iconic 1956 Phonosuper SK4 audio system, designed with Gugelot and nicknamed Snow White's Coffin for its white metal casing and Perspex hood. Aided by technological innovations, such as improved plastics and transistors, Rams introduced a clarity, neutrality and sophistication to the market, using a largely monochrome palette. Rams would later codify his approach to design in ten principles, the most famous of which was: 'Good design is as little design as possible.' Simplicity and purity were pursued over complication, with the aspiration that each product should be intuitive and even self-explanatory to the user.

Going professional

A combination of internal and external pressures saw the closure of Ulm in 1968, while, following its sale to Gillette the previous year, Braun soon bowed to market pressures and introduced colour into its product range, much to Rams's displeasure. By then, however, good design had been installed as the establishment line, with new state-backed organizations founded to improve standards, education and exports. These included Britain's Council of Industrial Design and West Germany's Council for Design, along with powerful professional bodies such as the Industrial Designers Society of America.

Apple of his eye

When looking for a contemporary equivalent of Dieter Rams, it is hard to see past Jony Ive, the British designer who joined Steve Jobs' Apple in 1992 and oversaw some of the most sensational design projects of the era, from the iMac to the iPhone. United by the 'as little design as possible' mantra, the influences are clear. One need only look at classic Braun products like the T3 pocket radio of 1958 or the ET44 and ET66 calculators produced 20 years later, to see how they influenced the design of the iPod and the iPhone calculator respectively. Ive's designs for Apple are the perfect extension of the good design ethos into the 21st century, confirmed by his own assertion that Rams's work is 'beyond improvement'.

Increasingly, the professional title of 'designer' pushed aside that of 'industrial artist', while the discipline attracted greater prestige and authority, along with copious literature. Nor was the phenomenon confined to Europe and North America – Japan was a hotbed of design excellence, with companies such as Matsushita, Canon and Toshiba hardwiring great design into their in-house teams.

Other voices

Gradually, however, disapproval crept in. Fatigue with the relentless top-down imposition of a single aesthetic resulted in the increasing embrace of the forms and fashions of popular culture in the 1960s. There was also criticism of the narrow definition of functionalism proposed in these 'universal' designs, which passed over broader social, psychological and cultural aspects, as well enviromental impacts. Victor Papanek became a spokesperson for the doubters in the 1970s, opening his book, *Design for the Real World*, with the words: 'There are professions more harmful than industrial design, but only a very few of them.' He believed that the world needed to move on from its Bauhaus inspirations of half a century earlier: 'As socially and morally involved designers, we must address ourselves to the needs of a world with its back to the wall.' Many listened, but not everyone. Despite ever-increasing invention and variety, and widespread recognition of the importance of self-expression and self-reflection, 'good design' remains the default option in the design industry today.

The condensed idea
Less, but better

22 Mid-century Modern

Much of the Modernist design around us today, particularly in our homes, falls into the 'mid-century' category, a style that emerged and reached a mass market in 15 short years after World War II, only acquiring its name in the 1980s. Given Modernism's meagre success beforehand, this widespread popularity was a dramatic turnaround. Previously, contemporary furniture had been viewed as elitist, expensive and alienating, suitable only for a liberal intelligentsia. Now, it was aspirational and increasingly affordable for all.

From war to wallpaper

This change partly came about owing to World War II itself. Materials and labour were in short supply, ensuring new products took simpler forms that required less of both. Fresh technologies emerged to maximize the potential of available materials and create new ones, often for military purposes. And, by the end of the war, a new mindset had emerged, one that aspired to a remodelled social contract, and to actively shape a better future. When constructing new homes to replace those destroyed by conflict, or investing in new production lines, a return to the past seemed absurd.

These new and refurbished homes – often apartments in Europe – adopted a clean and cleanable style. Modernist innovations were adopted by both construction industries and consumers, the latter slowly gaining in confidence and income as the war receded. With reduced working hours and shifts in social norms, the domestic environment gained importance and investment as a place of self-expression and self-realization. Old-fashioned features such as dado rails and cornices were lost, fitted kitchens with modern appliances were increasingly common, as were open-plan living areas, slimline heating and, in the United States, air-conditioning.

This new domestic vision was sold in popular magazines such as Britain's *Ideal Home*, America's *House Beautiful* and France's *Art & Décoration*. It was also showcased in cyclical exhibitions such as Ideal Home and Better Living, and was made visible and seductive on television (increasingly the focus of the room rather than the fireplace). As a result, indoor plants, room dividers and blinds all grew in popularity, as did bright wallpapers and screen-printed fabrics, both boasting fresh, modern patterns. And, of course, space-efficient, lightweight, modular furniture was a perfect fit, conveniently sold in coordinated ranges to be built up over time.

The American way

Mid-century was a broad church. In the United States, the appeal of Scandinavia's 'humane' Modernism, nurtured by pre-war figures such as Alvar Aalto and Børge Mogensen, loomed large. A longstanding reputation for high-quality workmanship in natural materials was furthered by beautiful, craft-oriented designs by Hans Wegner and Finn Juhl, while associations with socially egalitarian ideals proved highly attractive to US consumers with Modernist inclinations. The Nordic countries were not shy of harnessing these assumptions, coming together to organize the massive Design in Scandinavia exhibition that toured the United States from 1954, comprising some 700 exhibits, attracting more than 650,000 visitors, and forging a market for decades to come.

Homegrown Modernism in the United States took a more adventurous form, facilitated by European emigres in design education, and by committed furniture companies such as Knoll and Herman Miller. Charles and Ray Eames developed an 'organic design' that embraced the principles of European Modernism, tempered with a lightness of touch, bright colours and curvaceous forms. They harnessed new materials such as fibreglass and 3D-moulded plywood (both evolved for aircraft manufacture during the war) to create delightful modern furniture, some of it suitable for mass production, some more luxurious. Others, such as their friend Eero

> To create surroundings that satisfy the needs of modern man, and simply and naturally fulfil practical and aesthetic requirements. . .this has been our ideal, and, however imperfect the result, this ideal has inspired us.
> Design in Scandinavia catalogue, 1954

Saarinen and their mentor George Nelson, followed suit, the former with his super-comfortable Womb chair in a reinforced fibreglass adapted from shipbuilding, the latter with perennially inventive designs such as his Ball Clock and with commissions as a director at Herman Miller, including classic pieces from Isamu Noguchi and Harry Bertoia.

Inventing a style

All countries took their own route through mid-century, often backed by US money, usually aspiring to American lifestyles, and always competing for 'modern' status on the international stage. The most successful was Italy, reinventing itself from war-scarred country to the world's most stylish, aided by the international Milan Triennale and championed by the highbrow *Domus* magazine. Existing somewhere between artisanal and industrial in production and aesthetics, this new style aspired to beautify everything 'from the spoon to the city', in the words of architect and *Domus* editor Ernesto Rogers. Designer Gio Ponti stood supreme, combining tradition and modernity in his iconic Superleggera chair, and even bringing the latter to the bathroom with his award-winning Zeta suite. Most influential, however, was Marco Zanuso's Lady armchair, which embraced the production line with its foam-rubber padding and structural assembly, yet provided both comfort and allure.

With less pronounced results, similar trajectories can be traced in Brazil, Japan, France and beyond. In Eastern bloc countries, such as the former Czechoslovakia and Poland, for instance, mid-century design was embraced for its aesthetics and affordability, but also as a witness to an egalitarian, forward-looking society. In the United Kingdom, the Festival of Britain was held to celebrate the centenary of the Great Exhibition in 1951, unleashing a contemporary 'festival' style on both manufacturers and public, with celebrity couple Robin and Lucienne Day contributing furnishings and fabrics respectively. But, as in the US, Scandinavian design proved hugely popular, with a quarter of modern Danish cabinet making – all teak, rosewood and sinuous lines – heading to consumers in the United Kingdom.

The measure of success

Throughout the 1950s and well beyond, many manufacturers remained wedded to their existing aesthetics, markets and production lines. And many consumers preferred those traditional forms, taking comfort in the past, or unable to afford the upgrade. In Germany, for instance, heavy Gelsenkirchen Baroque furniture gained popularity in the late 1950s – when surveyed, 60 per cent of German women preferred such traditional furniture, with only 30 per cent opting for a gentle Swedish-style Modernism. In the United States, a 'frontier style' came into vogue at around the same time, and even in Italy the furniture industry clung to an antique style that Ernesto Rogers decried as 'Cantu Chippendale'. Part of Mid-century Modern's success can certainly be ascribed to its adoption in schools, offices and hospitals rather than homes, regarded as efficient, lightweight, affordable and hygienic. And its ascendancy soon led to inevitable backlashes against a government-backed 'conspiracy of good taste' – Pop was just around the corner in art, music and design. But this was definitely Modernism that actually worked for people – and, as its prevalence in homes today proves, it still does.

The condensed idea
A liveable modernity

23 Swiss Style

Rational Modernism still flourishes in many fields, but perhaps most of all in typography and graphic design. Taking shape in Switzerland in the 1940s and 1950s, it transformed these sectors, such that Swiss Style remains the default for many functions – an endurance, and provenance, epitomized by one typeface: Helvetica.

The pre-history of a style

Many of the components of Swiss Style coalesced in the 1920s. Early Bauhaus publications featured expressive layouts and eccentric typefaces, but these retrograde tendencies were ushered out by László Moholy-Nagy upon his arrival in 1923, when sans serifs were imposed as standard practice. However, his belief that 'the new typography is a simultaneous experience of vision and communication' led to idiosyncratic layouts with exaggerated asymmetry, expanses of blank space and prolific use of black rules to regulate the grid. Typefaces were geometric, speaking of the machine age, but of dubious legibility. Some were lowercase only, such as the futuristic Universal by Herbert Bayer, who asked, 'Why do we write and print with two alphabets? We do not speak with a capital A and a small a.'

This New Typography was given rigour by German designer Jan Tschichold. In his book of the same name, published in 1928, he prescribed strict principles around using sans-serif fonts, grids, photomontage, asymmetry and blank space, rejecting the stylized forms of Bauhaus typefaces, and even the softened geometries of Paul Renner's Futura. Instead, he championed 19th-century Grotesk typefaces, with their pared-back sans-serif letterforms designed for a wide range of sizes and applications, and with no particular aesthetic ambition.

Coming together

Denounced as a cultural Bolshevist, Tschichold emigrated to neutral Switzerland in 1933. There, he moved away from his previous severity, but others in the country assumed the mantle, including Bauhaus-trained designers Max Bill and Theo Ballmer, and students of pioneering Zurich-based designer Ernst Keller, such as Armin Hofmann and Josef Müller-Brockmann. Their evolution of, and propagandizing for, new graphics in the post-war period resulted in the term 'Swiss Style', in part due to the aura of rationality and prudence engendered by the country's wartime neutrality: Switzerland seemed an appropriate location for the emergence of a universal aesthetic.

The authoritative magazine *Neue Grafik*, of which Müller-Brockmann was an editor, advocated a strict design regime, with orthogonal grids, two font sizes, and horizontal text ranged left, all in pursuit of a mathematical precision that could generate both balance and tension. On posters and magazine covers, surprisingly lyrical arrangements were achieved with asymmetric layouts combining type, graphic elements, coloured blocks and photographs in complex arrangements. Basel-based designers such as Armin Hofmann, Emil Ruder and Karl Gerstner proved particularly effective in their more flexible application of the style to print marketing.

In keeping with Tschichold's preferences, Max Bill employed an anonymous sans-serif typeface released in 1896 by the Berthold Type Foundry, Akzidenz Grotesk, and other designers followed his lead. Witnessing its rise, the foundry Haas commissioned its own proprietary version, Helvetica, which was soon the foremost typeface of Swiss Style. More adventurous, and almost as successful, was the elegant Univers by Adrian Frutiger, which systematized the often confused provision of type weights and widths.

International impact

Max Bill returned to Germany in 1952 to take the helm at the Ulm School of Design – the inheritor of the Bauhaus mantle – bringing Swiss Style with him. It chimed perfectly with the school's highly intellectual approach, resulting in such wonderfully concise designs as Anton Stankowski's logo for Deutsche Bank and Otl Aicher's identities for airline Lufthansa and consumer brand Braun. Most famous is Aicher's work as lead designer for the 1972 Munich Olympics, including its pictograms formed from 45-degree angles and basic shapes. In other European countries, the embrace tended to be hesitant, with pharmaceutical companies, public institutions and transport infrastructure most enthusiastic, whether Benno Wissing's Akzidenz Grotesk-inspired signage for Amsterdam Schiphol Airport, or Design Research Unit's identity for British Rail. Due to its proximity, Italy experienced a flood of Swiss designers, leading to Max

Released in 1957, Max Miedinger's Neue Haas Grotesk met with immediate success. Clean, neutral and legible at any size, it was loosely derived from the Haas Type Foundry's own vintage Grotesk font, answering a widespread desire for a versatile universal typeface to replace, yet respect, Akzidenz Grotesk. Renamed Helvetica as a marketing ploy in 1960, it remains enormously popular today, and barely betrays its age, even if its lack of innovation, charm and a convincing italic have met with criticism. With Helvetica's successful transition into the digital age, its own documentary, and its dominance of the T-shirt market, such carping feels trivial. As Adrian Frutiger put it: 'Helvetica is the jeans, and Univers the dinner jacket. Helvetica is here to stay.'

Meet the cast:

ABCD EFGHIJK LMNOP QRSTUV WXYZ

Now see the movie:

Helvetica

A documentary film by Gary Hustwit

Huber's celebrated work for Olivetti, and also produced its own master in Massimo Vignelli. In France, acceptance for Swiss Style – seen as dogmatic, graceless and even totalitarian compared to its more artistic offerings – came as late as the 1980s, thus Adrian Frutiger had to be imported to provide signage at Paris's two main airports.

American graphic designers took a more liberal approach. Talents such as Paul Rand and Alvin Lustig felt able to adopt and adapt the style, stretching or breaking its tenets with illustrative elements and playfully cropped photographs. In the corporate context, it achieved more direct impact, for instance in Rand's famed logo for IBM, Tom Geismar and Eliot Noyes's colourful identity for Mobil, and Massimo Vignelli's American Airlines logo. The decision to commission Vignelli to overhaul the New York Subway's signage in 1966 proved once more that Swiss Style was ideally suited to providing guidance in confusing, crowded spaces.

The condensed idea
A universal style for a modern world

24 **UX Design**

User Experience Design, or UX Design, is a broad term, covering, as you might expect, the usability of a product or service, and whether it meets the user's needs, but encompassing more. Its guru, Don Norman, who worked at Apple in the 1990s, states that 'the first requirement for an exemplary user experience is to meet the exact needs of the customer, without fuss or bother', but also believes that it's vital to create products 'that are a joy to own, a joy to use'. To achieve this, they should merge 'multiple disciplines, including engineering, marketing, graphical and industrial design, and interface design'. In short, UX Design encompasses 'all aspects of the end-user's interaction with the company, its services and its products'.

Experiencing the telephone

It's an approach, and a mindset, that can be applied to pretty much anything – a book, a car, a moisturizer – but when mentioned today it's usually in a digital context, not a physical one. As an example, it's worth taking a closer look at one product that spans both: the telephone. Early examples tended to have messy forms, a result of being assembled out of multiple parts. In 1931, the Norwegian artist Jean Heiberg (who studied under Matisse) took advantage of a new material, Bakelite, to design a sleek, sculptural, all-in-one telephone casing for telecommunications company Ericsson. The result was quick to produce, hygienic, and felt comfortable and warm in the hand. American industrial designer Henry Dreyfuss appropriated the design for Bell Labs in the late 1930s, eventually developing it into the Model 500 in 1953. The latter drew on extensive research into face measurements, shoulder shapes and usage habits, and it pretty much defined the telephone for the following few decades. Its light, gently curving handset was designed to be cradled in the neck, freeing the hands, while its transparent dial, with numbers placed around the circumference, sped up dialling. In addition, its unassuming form was intended to sit politely and prettily in domestic

> We must design for the way people behave, not for how we would wish them to behave.
>
> Don Norman, *Living with Complexity*, 2010

interiors. For Dreyfuss, 'When the point of contact between the product and the people becomes a point of friction, then the [designer] has failed. On the other hand, if people are made safer, more comfortable, more eager to purchase, more efficient – or just plain happier – by contact with the product, then the designer has succeeded.' Additional happiness was provided by the introduction of colour options the following year, then in 1959 a compact 'feminine' alternative, the Princess, with a backlit dial, sold under the banner, 'It's small. . .it's lovely. . .it lights'.

The arrival of digital telephony in the 1960s, and the consequent replacement of dials with keypads, proved a mixed blessing. Norman, in his classic book *The Design of Everyday Things* (1988), lamented complex telephone systems that crammed an ever-increasing range of features – conference calls, call transfers, automatic callback and so on – onto 12 unremarkable buttons. These offered few visual clues as to their use, requiring hefty, impenetrable paper manuals to understand. Norman pointed out that such frustrations should not be categorized as our own shortcomings, but those of designers who decline to engage with their users, so develop products that fail to communicate with them. In contrast, a successful product should express its purpose and operations clearly, and give immediate, comprehensible feedback. And it should achieve this in a seamless fashion, so it feels intuitive, logical, almost inevitable.

Beyond the physical

Strangely, despite being almost inconceivably more powerful than those early systems, today we carry around in our pockets machines that achieve just that. The success of smartphones in employing graphical user interfaces and touchscreens to create intuitive experiences is astonishing. We expect to pick them up and understand their operation immediately. They are populated with apps that employ shared visual and gestural languages, giving us control over an extraordinary range of other functions. These descendants of the telephone aren't just user-friendly objects with user-friendly interfaces. They are a service as much as a product, existing within, and providing access to, an entire universe.

So where does UX Design end? Norman himself has said that the concept's penetration across all aspects of design, existing in a

Graphical user interfaces

If you ask about the best of contemporary UX Design, you'll usually be pushed towards the all-singing platform of a leading tech brand. Each of these stands on the shoulders of the pioneering graphical user interfaces, or GUIs, developed from the late 1960s onwards. With their visuals representing file structures, functions and feedback, including desktops, windows, icons, buttons and menus, they offered a mental model that soon became intrinsic to our interactions with the digital world and, as a result, the physical world. A basic form of the GUI was revealed at 'the mother of all demos', given in San Francisco by Stanford Research Institute professor Douglas Engelbart, when he also unveiled the first mouse (pictured). The idea of a simplified visual interface for underlying software code was taken up by Xerox in the 1970s, then developed by Apple in the early 1980s, with drag-and-drop functionality added along the way. GUIs have had a transformative impact on the accessibility of computing and, following the increased access to touchscreens from the 2000s, have become even more powerful and intuitive, largely leaving behind such visual metaphors as windows and introducing haptic feedback. They enable access to an inexhaustible world of content and customization, such that it is almost impossible to imagine life without them.

somewhat competitive relationship with other buzzy terms – brand design, interaction design, human-centred design and so on – has resulted in the term 'starting to lose its meaning'. In addition, a seamless, or even joyful, experience for the mass of users does not necessarily equate to good design. To revert to smartphones, only now are much-needed features ensuring accessibility for all being introduced, and perhaps the most effective of all the experiences, and one offering particularly impactful feedback – social media – targets, cultivates and capitalizes on the worst versions of ourselves, across all spheres of our lives, from the personal to the political. Once a discipline claims all design to itself, it needs to take responsibility for the results.

The condensed idea
Putting joy into the design experience

25 Design Museums

I t might seem strange to classify design museums as an idea, but they've been hugely influential in developing modern understandings of design, popularizing it as an aesthetic proposition and lifestyle aspiration and promoting it as a problem-solving and critical tool. As such, they are far more than accumulations of decorative objects – a role played by royal collections past and present. Instead, they strive to encapsulate and express changes in culture, technology and society.

Breaking ground

There isn't much dispute about the world's first design museum. The success of London's Great Exhibition in 1851 resulted in £5,000 of its profits being used to buy a selection of exhibits considered representative of 'correct design'. This coalesced into a 'Museum of Manufactures', intended as a practical tool for the improvement of Britain's industrial output, ensuring that companies could compete on a world market. In 1857, as the South Kensington Museum, it found a permanent home just south of the Crystal Palace's original location. By 1899, when it gained its current name – the Victoria and Albert Museum – the collections had expanded to encompass almost all arts, mediums, nations and eras.

> An ace caff with quite a nice museum attached.
>
> Victoria and Albert Museum advert, 1988

Henry Cole, the civil servant who played a pivotal role in the realization of the Great Exhibition, was its first director. He felt that the museum should act as a 'schoolroom for everyone', installing gas lighting so collections could remain open until 10 o'clock two nights a week, as well as a 'refreshment room', in the conviction that 'the evening opening of public museums may furnish a powerful antidote to the gin palace'. Through an encounter with beauty and utility, he believed, the empty promises of luxury and vanity would be exposed. Products displaying excessive ornamentation and a lack of harmony between their decoration and function (a failure causing particular angst) were gathered in a 'False Principles Gallery' – it closed after two weeks when manufacturers complained.

International appeal

Seeking to emulate the Victoria and Albert Museum's prestige and purpose, similar institutions spread rapidly across the world's capitals and beyond, often involving large-scale purchases at international exhibitions or transfers of royal collections. Vienna, Berlin, Oslo, Paris, Buenos Aires, New York, Krakow, Prague, Chicago and any number of other cities have museums or collections inspired by its example, many founded by local industrial or decorative arts societies. Some focused on artistic display or national styles, others on instruction. Leipzig's Museum für Kunsthandwerk, founded in 1874, was particularly robust in its goals, seeking 'to take action against the archaic ways and pathetic mediocrity' of German industry. In contrast, Sydney's new Museum of Applied Arts and Sciences had, in 1879, the less aggressive ambition of creating an institution 'of interest and lasting service to the mass of the population'. As fashion, politics and personnel fluctuated over the decades, the mission of the design museum fluctuated in turn.

Going modern

Although the Victoria and Albert Museum came first, it hasn't always guided understandings of what a design museum can be. The Neue Sammlung in Munich, which became a state museum in 1925, is usually cited as the first to commit to Modernist industrial design as its key concern. Four years later, New York's Museum of Modern Art embraced all the arts, aspiring to 'encourage and develop the study of the modern art and the application of such arts to manufacture and public life'. Under controversial architect and connoisseur Philip Johnson, its Department of Architecture organized the Modern Architecture exhibition of 1932, showcasing the International style, and Machine Art two years later, exploring 'the formal ideals of beauty that have become the major style concepts of our time'.

By the 1950s, the New York museum had become a champion of contemporary industrial design, holding a series of Good Design displays – a collaboration with Chicago wholesalers Merchandise Mart – as well as groundbreaking exhibitions devoted to automobiles as 'hollow, rolling sculpture', and to modern designs from Italian manufacturer Olivetti, celebrating the latter for their beauty and utility, while praising the company's 'organization of all the visual aspects of an industry, unified under a single high standard of taste'. By 1958, Braun's exquisitely styled electrical appliances had taken up residence in its permanent collections.

This championing of functional design by the major art institution of the world's economic superpower was widely noted. A consequent shift took place in the 1960s, in museums around the globe that were dedicated to the decorative arts, which saw a new emphasis on contemporary products and international trends, and sometimes a new institutional title. Ironically, one result was to reduce the focus on affordable mass-produced objects, in favour of the expense, prestige and pretension of 'high design', hastened by donations from industry and collectors, and by the professionalization of the design industry.

In 1905, Amersterdam's Stedelijk Museum had displayed utilitarian items appropriate for working-class flats in its Art for the People display. By 1966, its 50 Years of Sitting exhibition was promoting design as a sophisticated intellectual endeavour mirroring developments in art and society. Similarly, in its 1955 Elements of Design show, the Cooper Hewitt in New York addressed the evolution of design practice and education by dividing the 96 exhibits by colour, surface, line, rhythm and form.

The design museum today

Design museums aren't going away, nor is their expanding compass. Through an intense examination of an object – any object – the ties that bind the modern world can be revealed. Those could relate to the availability of raw materials or to global trade, or to developments in technology or infrastructure. They can reflect political and economic trends, or social and cultural shifts – or all of the above. And that same object can cast light in more intangible ways, suggesting contemporary motivations, morals, identities and conceptions of beauty. Or just current hair styles. As a result, for many design museums, the quality of an object now takes second place to the story it can tell.

In practice, however, financial realities often mean that the prime focus has moved from innovative displays based around collections – frequently the museum's original purpose – to temporary exhibitions bringing in sponsorship and sales. Expanding on the tentative efforts of their predecessors, there is also a necessary focus on commercial collaborations, refreshments and retail. In parallel, major department

In 1934, Philip Johnson, curator of architecture at the Museum of Modern Art, New York, unveiled 400 everyday objects, domestic and industrial, on pedestals of walnut and cedar, with minimal text to distract from their perfection – although price lists were provided. Test tubes, telescopes, ball bearings, propellors, cigarette lighters, a carpet sweeper and one Bauhaus chair were selected for usefulness and beauty 'regardless of whether their fine design was intended by artist or engineer or was merely the unconscious result of the efficiency compelled by mass production'. Its success led to a new name – the Department of Architecture and Industrial Design – and an unexpected follow-up, a tenement from a demolished New York slum, complete with the final occupants' possessions. Design was heading in new directions.

stores are increasingly launching their own ambitious exhibition programmes. The two typologies have long been battling it out as the pre-eminent location for the display and consumption of design – encroaching on each other's territories in this way makes perfect sense as they continue this fundamental struggle.

The condensed idea
Design on display

26 Infographics

I n the simplest terms, infographics can be described as visual representations of data or other information intended to communicate ideas or knowledge in a swift and accessible way. Designing an infographic – a compound of 'information' and 'graphic' coined in the 1970s – can be a complex undertaking. Each requires the evolution of a distinct visual form tailored to the precise information – and the particular story – that it needs to convey. Despite their overwhelming prevalence today, there is an argument that the earliest infographics are cave paintings, some dating back over 40,000 years, that provided information about local fauna (particularly predators) and natural features long before the advent of written language.

The mind's eye

In our own data-driven era, we have never been confronted by so much information, but an elegant infographic can aid its digestibility, helping our brains to absorb material visually – whether or not it is entirely accurate. It is thought that something like half of the human brain is dedicated to processing visual functions. In the four or five minutes needed to read this short essay, the brain can process some 3,000 visual images. As a result, communicating a point quickly and efficiently can be achieved far more readily with an infographic than an extended written passage. But designing a truly effective one is a highly skilled art, involving a balance between the visual itself, the raw data underpinning the infographic, and the informational framing of that data – the story that it is intended to tell.

A great infographic will have immediate visual appeal, while ensuring its message is both easily comprehensible and retained by the viewer. It's a fairly narrow band of ambitions, yet there are myriad forms that the most successful ones can take. No US election night would be complete without a map of the United States coloured in the red of the Republicans and the blue of the Democrats, providing a perfect visualization of what can often seem a complicated electoral system. Compare that with the iconic London Underground map, first conceived by Harry Beck in 1931 – wilfully geographically inaccurate, it serves as a spell-binding, colour-exploiting conceptualization of information involving multiple transport lines, hundreds of stations, their positions relative to each other, their crossover points and connections, along with a wealth of further information. Now compare both of those with Otl Aicher's magnificent pictograms for the 1972 Munich Olympic Games that graphically represented each sport and facilitated the movement of vast numbers of competitors and spectators safely between venues and sessions. Each is a brilliant infographic, and entirely unlike the others.

A history of data visualization

The art of infographics has been a long time in development: from early cave paintings we might jump several thousand millennia to the ancient Egyptians, whose hieroglyphs have echoes of Aicher's much later works. Or we could explore the maps and astronomical charts that since antiquity have striven to make sense of the world and the night sky in highly simplified two-dimensional (and, latterly, three-dimensional) form. However, it was not until 1786 that Scottish engineer and economist William Playfair published *The Commercial and Political Atlas*, utilizing innovative visual representations including bar charts, line graphs and what would become known as histograms. Playfair is also credited with inventing the pie chart 15 years later, supporting his recent investiture as 'the godfather of infographics'. Famously, his work helped disprove a widely-held theory that wage increases were driving up wheat prices, leaving popular and political opinion no choice but to bend in front of the evidence. Data, Playfair argued, should 'speak to the eyes', since they are 'the best judge of proportion, being able to estimate it with more quickness and accuracy than any other of our organs'.

The potency of a well-hewn infographic was proven time and again in the 19th century. In the 1850s, for example, the physician John Snow pinpointed the source of a deadly cholera outbreak in London by plotting the incidence data onto a map. The following decade, across the Atlantic, the US Coast Survey published a large infographic map, almost a metre wide, depicting the density of slave populations in the southern states, exposing the distribution of a system that kept almost four million people in bondage. Consulted by Abraham Lincoln, the map was to influence Unionist military strategy during the Civil War.

Perhaps one of Florence Nightingale's lesser-known achievements is her contribution to the development of the infographic, especially with her so-called 'rose diagrams'. These were a variation on the pie chart, each slice representing deaths in a different month of the Crimean War. Every slice was colour-coded (blue for death by disease, red for death from wounds and black for other causes), and extended further the more deaths there were. Their gruesome revelation, clear for all to see, was how many more soldiers were dying from disease than as a result of combat – proof that Nightingale was correct to champion better hygiene in field hospitals. Her brilliant infographic aimed, she suggested, 'to affect thro' the Eyes what we fail to convey to the public through their word-proof ears'.

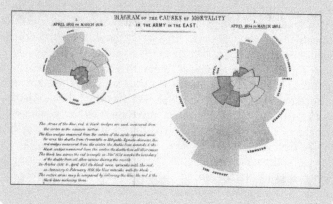

The modern age

It was inevitable that the commercial world would eventually grasp the form's economic potential. A full 16 years before Harry Beck unleashed his Tube map on the world, another artist employed by London Underground, Alfred Leete, designed an infographic poster that compared six modes of transport to reveal the Tube's speed advantage. The use of infographics has been a staple of the ad business ever since. In the 1930s, there were efforts to standardize the language of infographics at the Gesellschafts- und Wirtschaftsmuseum in

Vienna under Otto Neurath. He employed a team of artists, including Gerd Arntz, Peter Alma and Augustin Tschinkel, to develop Isotype – the International System of Typographic Picture Education – with its own standard symbols and rules about the representation of data, which were disseminated internationally and proved influential to future infographic designers.

The print media took a while to catch up with these developments, but by the 1970s, graphic designer Peter Sullivan was using the form to elucidate complex stories in *The Sunday Times*, prompting a trend that spread to other newspapers. In the 1980s, Edward Tufte established himself as the leading theoretician of infographics, publishing *The Visual Display of Quantitative Information* in 1982. Incidentally, he considered a statistical graph created in 1869 by French engineer Charles Joseph Minard depicting Napoleon's losses in his Russian campaign of 1812 as the greatest infographic of them all.

The internet has inordinately increased the scope and appetite for infographics, with software programs allowing for their easy production in three dimensions as well as two. The only thing quicker than modern data production is the rate at which this information is thrown at audiences. With the virtual-reality revolution at full throttle, it is likely only a matter of time before infographics evolve to float in front of our eyes. Whether that will make lives richer in knowledge as well as mere data, only time will tell.

The condensed idea
An infographic paints a thousand words

27 Pop Design

Employing the 'pop' tag conjures up visions of captivating music, bright colours, bold fashions and the explosion of popular culture, all tied up with social freedoms forged in the wake of World War II. Applied to art, it denotes a radical new aesthetic that evolved in the 1950s and 1960s, gleefully drawing on 'the everyday', from packaging and technology to comic books and posters. Blurring the distinction between 'high art' and 'low culture' and playing to its own improvised rules, it luxuriated in its refusal to conform to precedent and tradition. Whether Pop Art strove principally to celebrate the throwaway culture that blossomed amid America's post-war capitalist boomtimes, or to critique it, remains moot. Its lifespan was relatively short, but its impact on subsequent artistic production and consumption has been long-lasting. Its effect on design, however, is a more nuanced tale.

The design crossover

Pop Art was birthed in the United Kingdom, with Eduardo Paolozzi's 1947 collage, *I Was a Rich Man's Plaything*, bringing together a selection of popular-culture artefacts to become arguably its first major work. Paolozzi was a member of the Independent Group, whose 1956 exhibition This is Tomorrow marked the wider arrival of the movement, spearheaded by Richard Hamilton's seminal collage, *Just What Is It That Makes Today's Homes So Different, So Appealing?*, depicting a mid-century living room crammed with consumer products and motifs, and populated by a bodybuilder and a burlesque star, all cut from a convenient stash of American magazines. The following year, he offered this definition of Pop Art: 'Popular (designed for a mass audience), Transient (short-term solution), Expendable (easily forgotten), Low cost, Mass produced, Young (aimed at youth), Witty, Sexy, Gimmicky, Glamorous, Big Business.'

The Independent Group also included husband-and-wife architects Peter and Alison Smithson, who exhibited their strikingly curvaceous House of the Future prototype – seemingly moulded plastic, in fact plywood, plaster and paint – at London's Ideal Home Show in 1956. It offered a vision of an ultramodern life of mobility, technology and consumerism, with a self-cleaning bath and multiple remote controls,

Joe Colombo

Artist, architect and industrial designer, Joe Colombo was a visionary of Pop design over his short life, dying in 1971 on his 41st birthday. Prolific, energetic and iconoclastic, he was responsible for a catalogue of revolutionary designs, from curvaceous, colourful table lamps to alluring storage trolleys, all embracing flexible forms, modern materials and bold finishes. His 1969 Tubo chair, for instance, was a modular seat constructed from four hollow cylinders of PVC connected by tubular steel, covered with polyurethane foam and fabric. Its materials were all individually cheap but its design was decidedly space age. Colombo breached the divide between artist and technician, creating futuristic furniture that would not look out of place in the science fiction that frequently inspired him.

forecast to arrive in 1981. Between them, the Independent Group's members engineered a radical fracture with dominant design culture, paving the way for the emergence of avant-garde architectural groups such as Archigram in the early 1960s.

However, Pop achieved the peak of its fame in the United States, with several of its leading artists – Andy Warhol, Roy Lichtenstein, Jasper Johns, Richard Artschwager, James Rosenquist, Robert Indiana – becoming household names. Although individually distinctive, they were united in a broad rejection of high culture and an acknowledgement of the popular, raising familiar motifs to the rank of art. In part a response to the austerity and elitism of abstraction, Pop Art was also a rebellion of the young against the imposition of uniform standards in culture, although it swiftly joined the traditional art ecosystem. In a similar manner, designers working under Pop's influence undertook a fundamental rethink of functionalism, dramatically expanding design's scope.

Plastic possibilities

In some ways, Pop design emerged out of the pre-existing logic of the luxury design industry, with its constant pursuit of innovative, eye-catching new styles, and of consequent financial rewards – Pop just had a raft of new materials with which to achieve these ends. Such futuristic plastics as polymethyl methacrylate (PMMA), polypropylene and polyurethane allowed for the creation of seamless new objects, apparently immaculate but often, as in the case of inflatables, acting as emblems of a throwaway culture. A succession of trailblazers duly emerged. The Danish furniture and interior designer, Verner Panton, enjoyed an extraordinary career, his pioneering output including the iconic cantilevered S-Chair (the first chair to be made from a single piece of moulded plastic), and the exuberantly geometric Cone Chair. Another was the polymathic Italian designer Ettore Sottsass, who spent two decades at the technology giant Olivetti, before establishing the Memphis Group in 1980, co-opting Pop's bright colour palette, broad cultural references and sense of possibility.

> It will be a great day when furniture and cutlery design, to name but two, swing like the Supremes.
>
> Michael Wolff, *Journal of the Society of Industrial Artists*, 1965

The Italian scene

In 1961, the Salone del Mobile was launched to further promote Italy's furniture and furnishings industry, aspiring to preserve its global preeminence in cutting-edge design. In combination with the country's strong design networks, the fair proved a perfect set for groundbreaking figures with Pop sensibilities such as Joe Colombo (see box), the Castiglioni brothers, famed for their playful lighting designs, and Gaetano Pesce, whose output included the vacuum-packed UP5_6, a bulbous polyurethane lounge chair with attached ottoman resembling a ball and chain, commenting on women's position as prisoners in society.

This last was representative of the experimental Italian school of Anti-Design, of which Sottsass was also a leading figure. With its playful and inventive use of unexpected forms, materials and colours, it employed design to critique society rather than serve a function. Comprising radical collectives such as Archizoom, Superstudio, Gruppo Strum and Studio 65, and often abetted by Turin-based company Gufram, it drew on Surrealism and Pop Art to produce objects like Studio 65's Dalí-channelling Bocca sofa and its Capitello chair (a classical Ionic capital made from cheap foam rather than marble) or Gruppo Strum's Pratone chair, manufactured from polyurethane to resemble a patch of lawn. If it were needed, this rich period of creativity, in which art and design coalesced, was given official American blessing in 1972 with Italy: The New Domestic Landscape at New York's Museum of Modern Art.

Leaving the bright lights

Despite its basis in popular culture, there were always many different versions of Pop design, with its most elaborate expressions almost all destined for an elite audience. For many, Pop's main consequence was increased eclecticism – the bold colours, patterns and graphics on curtains and wallpapers were as likely to be Victorian patterns as contemporary ones. Bean bags and curvaceous polyurethane sofas made headway, but cheap plastic homewares and accessories were the real winners. By the mid-1970s, the game was virtually up. Pop had risen as a critical reaction to a paternalistic, uniform and slightly dull design culture first mooted in the 1930s, and a feeling that popular culture might offer a route to something more vibrant. But in the wake of economic shocks and oil crises, reality was biting again. In addition, plastic was growing more expensive and less environmentally desirable. Pop's iconic designs were relegated to the sets of science-fiction movies, while manufacturers introduced more pastoral, reflective and inexpensive styles for mass markets. Meanwhile, at its highest echelons, design culture was turning towards the wider intellectual horizons of Postmodernism. Pop's time in the sun had been brief, but its liberation of design's potential endured.

The condensed idea
Turning plastic into gold

28 Corporate Identity

A strong corporate identity – encompassing the ways in which a business projects itself, but also its inherent culture – is essential for the success of any modern enterprise. Achieving one, though, is a complex process, and many moving cogs are required to develop a consistent and trustworthy identity that connects with consumers and communicates an organization's values. Today, it involves all aspects of the business – tone-of-voice guidelines, brand stories and mission statements come with the territory. But a consumer's first interaction with a brand is typically visual. And, as US companies proved with impressive regularity in the 1960s, if you get your logo right – ideally as part of a total package with typography, colour schemes, graphics, perhaps uniforms and showrooms – the battle for hearts, minds and wallets is already part won.

Building a brand

Stamping marks is nothing new, but as more and more trade went national, then global, in the 19th century, the power of a strong brand became ever clearer. In the United States, Coca-Cola's dramatic script and colours were in place by the early 1890s, while in Britain – perhaps tellingly – the very first logo to be registered was the red triangle of Staffordshire brewers Bass in 1876, as visible in Édouard Manet's *A Bar at the Folies-Bergère* painted five years later. When looking for the first fully realized corporate identity, however, most turn to German electrical manufacturer Allgemeine Elektricitäts-Gesellschaft (AEG), and the work of industrial designer Peter Behrens who, as artistic consultant, oversaw all aspects of the company's design from 1907, from its kettles and streetlamps to its Berlin factory complex. Crucially, his remit also extended to developing material that would convey the essence of the company, including logos, publications and promotional materials, all with a consistent design aesthetic.

It didn't really catch on, although branding was clearly of increasing concern. In 1917, London Transport introduced a striking new roundel and typeface, both designed by typographer Edward Johnston. Rolled out across advertising and signage, then integrated into its new stations and bus stops as part of a brand-building embrace of progressive design, the roundel became the symbol of London's public transport, and of London. Over in the United States, Neil H McElroy, a junior executive at Procter & Gamble, introduced the concept of 'brand management' in 1931. Frustrated at competition between products within the company's portfolio, he proposed that individual brands act as independent entities, with dedicated teams and marketing budgets, as well as set target audiences, ensuring each manager would be intimate with one specific brand, thus equipped and accountable for its success.

Creating an identity

In the 1950s, things started to change. Global corporations needed an overarching identity – one that would work across the world, be durable and distinct, and convey modernity. As with much of post-war design, Modernism provided an answer with its promise of simplicity and universality. Clear sans-serif typefaces were soon pushing aside their florid predecessors, while striking geometrical

The power of a logo

A common thread that links many of the most successful logos is simplicity. Nike's 'swoosh' was breathed into life in 1971 by graphic designer Carolyn Davidson – then a student at Portland State University – who was paid a mere $35 fee for the job. She based her design on the wings of the eponymous Greek goddess, encapsulating a sense of athleticism and vigour. Quickly identifiable around the world, it established the company's identity in what proved a ferocious battle for the sportswear market, positioning the firm well against the likes of Adidas (with its own celebrated triple-stripe insignia). Offering a powerful mix of timelessness and motion, the Nike logo has proved indestructible, while Davidson received a belated reward of 500 shares after the company went public in 1980.

logos – some abstract, some with initials – were introduced. The effect was clean, scalable, modern and neutral, avoiding overt national references.

Despite its European origins, US companies proved particularly adept at employing Modernist design to generate a strong corporate identity. In 1952, New York's Museum of Modern Art held its Olivetti: Design in Industry exhibition, displaying everything from typewriters to photographs of its nursery schools 'to encourage American industries to follow the lead of this corporation in organizing all the visual aspects of the industry under a single high standard of taste'. The Italian manufacturer's wholesale Modernism did indeed prove inspiring, resulting in IBM's hiring of graphic designer Paul Rand to overhaul its own visual identity, with other major figures – Marcel Breuer and Charles and Ray Eames – brought in to refresh its architecture and products respectively. By 1956, Rand had created a design manual for IBM's use, including a crisp new 'continuity logo' in a heavy slab-serif font – as intended, it is still in use today, with horizontal bands added in 1972 for 'speed and dynamism'. To round things off, the leading architect of corporate America, Mies van der Rohe, was commissioned to design IBM's new global headquarters in 1966 – a sleek, sophisticated glass-and-steel tower, stamping the company's brand on the Chicago skies.

Good design is good business.
Thomas J Watson Jr, CEO, IBM, 1973

As the power of the corporate identity became clear, any self-respecting American company commissioned its own from a leading designer – Rand, Saul Bass, Massimo Vignelli, Chermayeff & Geismar and Lester Beall among them. Many of the resulting logos remain in service today. Tom Geismar's clean-cut Mobil identity, with its red 'O' symbolizing energy, was employed across signage, tankers, packaging, stationery – and even influenced the space-age circular canopies and cylindrical pumps of the petroleum giant's service stations. Firms in Europe soon followed suit. German state carrier Lufthansa, for instance, turned to the arbiters of 'good design' – the Ulm School of Design – for its new identity in 1962, with Otl Aicher generating a stylish colour palette, a modern Helvetica-inspired typeface and an updated crane logo. Keeping things simple has proven a trusted route for many identities since, whether Apple's partially munched apple (designed by Rob Janoff in 1977) or Google's unmistakable wordmark (designed by Ruth Kedar in 1999, using the Catull font created by Gustav Jaeger in the early 1980s). A brief flirtation with a more representational approach in the 2000s – the 3D sheen given to Paul Rand's United Parcel Services (UPS) logo for instance, or Instagram's lifelike Polaroid camera – has largely ebbed away, with the flat and abstract making its return.

Moving on

Corporate identity can be a precarious game though. McDonald's famous 'golden arches' – first incorporated into the company logo back in 1962 – is a design icon known across the planet. Although brilliant for brand recognition, this has also seen the symbol used as shorthand for globalization itself, not always to the company's advantage. *New York Times* columnist Thomas L Friedman, for example, posited his 'Golden Arches theory' based on the observation that no two nations sufficiently economically developed to support a McDonald's network have ever gone to war. The observation may be factually flawed, but that link between the McDonald's brand and global capitalism remains. Another layer of complexity has arisen from the ongoing explosion of social media, intensifying the demands of on-brand content creation, in terms of quantity, speed and quality, but also suitability across global markets, in order to avoid offence and the resulting backlash. Achieving a universal tone of voice, and a widely trusted corporate identity, is only going to get more difficult.

The condensed idea
Presenting an organization's best face

29 Minimalism

Minimalism is best known as an extreme version of abstract art reliant on the use of the simplest shapes and forms and the smallest possible range of materials and colours. It emerged in New York in the late 1950s, but its 'less is more' credo gained a foothold around the world. Its pared-back nature is less a gesture of denial than one of intentionality, eliminating unnecessary distraction to enhance the value of engagement with an object. Sometimes seen as a strike against consumerism, it prizes authenticity, and has come to encapsulate not just an aesthetic philosophy but an entire mindset. As a result, a figure such as the Japanese organizing consultant, Marie Kondo, can achieve global fame by promoting a Minimalist approach to interior design – and virtually all other aspects of life – as a means of achieving inner tranquillity and personal happiness.

Artistic origins

The economic boom in 1950s America saw consumerism flourish, but by the end of the decade, there were signs of weariness. A generation of young New York artists began to turn away from the multilayered complexities of Abstract Expressionism towards simpler forms, colours and textures, amid fears that the art scene had become stale and academic. This coincided with renewed interest in earlier movements, not least the Russian avant-garde. In 1962, Camilla Gray published the influential *The Great Experiment in Art: 1863–1922*, the first major English-language study of the Russian Constructivists and Suprematists, and works like Kazimir Malevich's *Black Square* (1915), composed of a black square on a white background, soon became touchstones. There was also renewed interest in the ready-mades of Marcel Duchamp, in which prefabrication distanced the art from its creator's biography, as well as in the strict geometry of De Stijl.

From this crucible of influences emerged the first generation of Minimalists, united in a pursuit of simplicity, its art shorn of multitudes of meanings and references. Among its leaders was Frank Stella, whose striped 'black paintings' marked a major staging post, and whose assertion that 'What you see is what you see' was adopted as the movement's unofficial mantra. Another of its pioneers –

although far from a fan of the Minimalist label – was Donald Judd, famous for his series of boxes crafted from various materials, who argued for artworks being 'specific objects' of inherent value without

> A simple box is really a pretty complicated thing.
> Donald Judd, 1966–67

any expectation of them representing some external reality. 'A shape, a volume, a colour, a surface is something itself,' he wrote. 'It shouldn't be concealed as part of a fairly different whole.'

Minimalism asserted its place in the artworld with the Primary Structures exhibition at New York's Jewish Museum in 1966, which featured works by Judd, Sol LeWitt, Dan Flavin, Robert Morris, Carl Andre and others. Andre's *Lever* was arguably the showstopper – 137 firebricks lined up on the floor as if a column had fallen. It was a challenge to visitors unused to art neither hung on a wall nor positioned on a pedestal, demanding an unprecedented type of interaction. In his 'Notes on Sculpture', Morris elucidated how the interpretation of Minimalist works relied on the viewer's intuition but also the conditions in which a work was seen – the artists took themselves out of the equation in terms of providing meaning, placing that responsibility firmly with the audience.

Away from the gallery

Despite its elevated status in art, Minimalism has a strange place in design, found on the cover of coffee-table books but rarely in the index of monographs, hovering uneasily between style and philosophy. The clean, elegant furniture of Marcel Breuer and Arne Jacobsen or the refined electronics of Dieter Rams and Jony Ive might reasonably be called 'minimal', but come from a Modernist tradition, with its ideals of functionality, simplicity, geometry, universalism and truth to materials. Their minimalism is a byproduct, albeit an appealing one.

There are, however, those who champion Minimalism as a design system, lifestyle and philosophy, with its extreme removal of the extraneous facilitating closer engagement with what really matters. The relatively obscure Italian designer A G Fronzoni is hailed as a pioneer. His sparse designs from the 1960s and 1970s included his Serie 64 furniture in tubular metal, in which ergonomics were rejected in favour of rectilinearity, as well as the supremely elegant Quadra

Minimalism may struggle when confronted with the mess of life, but it flourishes amid fantasies. In the 1960s, Roy Halston Frowick – Halston – took the fashion world by storm. The stars were his friends, from Andy Warhol to Liza Minnelli. Starting out as a milliner, he was responsible for Jackie Kennedy's beloved pillbox hat, which she wore to her husband's presidential inauguration in 1961. When Halston's first ready-to-wear collection appeared in 1969, it caused a sensation with its sophisticated Minimalism, framing wearers sympathetically without calling undue attention to them. He would tell *Vogue* of his quest to dispense with 'all of the extra details that didn't work – bows that didn't tie, buttons that didn't button, zippers that didn't zip, wrap dresses that didn't wrap. I've always hated things that don't work.'

wall lamp – a simple black square with light spilling out from behind. His views were trenchant: 'I detest everything that is superfluous, surplus, redundant, all forms of waste, not only of materials, labour or technology, but moral and ethical waste.'

As so often, it took art to give this attitude intellectual respectability. In the early 1970s, Donald Judd started to design simple straight-edged chairs, tables, benches and a bed in pine for himself, and in the 1980s, produced commercial metal equivalents, drawing on De Stijl and – like A G Fronzoni – the harmonious aesthetics and meditative traditions of Japan. Judd's approach to furniture overlapped with his earlier notion of the Specific Object: 'A work of art exists as itself; a chair exists as a chair itself. And the idea of a chair isn't a chair.'

Living Minimalism

The architect John Pawson – a prominent advocate of the movement – has said, 'Minimalism is not an architecture of self-denial, deprivation or absence: it is defined not by what is not there, but by the rightness of what is there and by the richness with which this is experienced.' When furniture takes simple abstract forms, expressing its essence rather than adapting to specific purposes or styles, it becomes a space apart from the world, allowing for pause, reflection and a fuller appreciation of life. Such serenity is hard to achieve in practice, thus Minimalism's entanglement with luxury, and with hotels. Stone bathtubs filled by a lone pipe, sinks sunk into marble slabs and wooden benches with folded white towels are all possible because a spacious suite is free of belongings, is cleaned and tidied every day and has carefully constructed built-in storage. In the domestic sphere, these conditions – and the associated mindfulness – tend to be possible only with wealth.

Among the designers often denoted 'Minimalist' are Jasper Morrison and Naoto Fukasawa, who together evolved the concept of Super Normal – anonymous objects stripped of specific identity or originality, existing in a heightened state of 'normality'. Morrison in particular is known for deliberately plain designs, often refinements of existing types, but with lasting value: 'I realized that certain less noticeable objects could over time become the object of daily choice by virtues of charm, stealth and efficiency.' It's an appealing philosophy, and possibly a means towards a less grandiose Minimalism, one that doesn't require a curated space, an affluent lifestyle and an interior designer to become achievable.

The condensed idea
Less is more

30 Postmodernism

Postmodernism has a reputation, on the one hand, of being flashy, pricey and slightly silly, and on the other of being deeply intellectual – a literary and artistic rejection of modern ideas about reason, knowledge, progress, language and truth. Its flowering in design turned out to be, unexpectedly, one of the most successful of its iterations, drawing closely on newly minted architectural theory, and in particular the work of Robert Venturi. Published in 1966, his *Complexity and Contradiction in Architecture* expressed exhaustion with the intellectual and aesthetic restrictions of Modernism, which was then being criticized for its negative impacts on American cities. In place of these constraints, Venturi embraced a diversity of forms and influences, and the artistic potential of ambiguity and contextualism: 'I am for messy vitality over obvious unity. I include the non sequitur and proclaim the duality. I am for richness of meaning rather than clarity of meaning: for the implicit function as well as the explicit function.' Or, as he more concisely put it, 'Less is a bore.'

Design goes Postmodern

Although most professional organizations and public institutions remained firmly focused on Modernist objects and ideologies in the 1960s, popular taste proved less tractable and, in Italy, even high design began to embrace complexity and contradiction. The emergence of flamboyant and futuristic youth-oriented products by such figures as Joe Colombo and Verner Panton went hand in hand with the sophisticated 'anti-design' of groups that included Archizoom and Superstudio, who sought to give the discipline greater political and cultural meaning, rejecting the exaggerated elegance associated with Italian style at the time.

These tendencies were taken to a new level by Milan-based Studio Alchimia, founded by Italian architect Alessandro Guerriero in 1976 with participation from superstar designers such as Alessandro Mendini, Paola Navone, Michele De Lucchi and Ettore Sottsass. As well as such provocative showpieces as Mendini's extravagant Proust armchair, which combined Rococo form and hand-painted pointillist decoration, Studio Alchimia also exhibited experimental 'banal' items such as footballs or carpet sweepers. These were transformed through alchemy – the application of colour, pattern, ornament and irony – into meaningful aesthetic objects that communicated on multiple levels, with 'no regret for the lost utopia' of Modernism. This pursuit of profound meaning through ornament drew on the literary study of semiotics – an investigation of visual and linguistic signs and symbols – which had been given new prominence and fashionability in the

Irrational sitting

The nine cartoon-like, laminated plywood chairs designed from 1978 by Robert Venturi and his partner in life and practice Denise Scott Brown for the American manufacturer Knoll together form one of the icons of Postmodernism. Each chair represents a historical style, from Chippendale to Gothic Revival to Biedermeier, in a flat, abstract manner, employing exaggerated silhouettes and often screen-printed pattern and painted decoration. The result is a witty, colourful celebration of style and technology – and a wry nod to Alvar Aalto's bentwood furniture – but not a practical sitting experience.

1950s by the publication of *Mythologies*, a collection of essays by French writer Roland Barthes.

The radical design collective Memphis Group, established in 1981 by Sottsass with De Lucchi, Mendini, Martine Bedin, Nathalie du Pasquier and others, took this approach a stage further. A dizzying diversity of styles, forms and patterns, including allusions to myth and spiritualism, and to popular culture and vernacular forms – a combination of 'high' and 'low' culture known as double-coding – was employed on everything from clocks and ceramics to fabric and furniture. Prevailing notions of taste and quality were rejected, along with the creative and emotional limitations of Modernism, in favour of expression, sensuality, irony and even vulgarity. Bold patterns were often applied to laminated MDF, chosen for its flat surfaces, evident cheapness and lack of pre-existing cultural references. The effect was to 'turn a piece of furniture into a complex system of communication', in the words of Memphis artistic director Barbara Radice.

> **Postmodernism is not a repetition of Modernism, but its transcendence, a questioning of the values it holds most sacred — objectivity, rationality and progress.**
> Charles Jencks, 1986

Unlike Studio Alchimia, Memphis aspired to at least some commercial reach, but with little success. Yet its influence, and that of the eloquent and multi-talented Sottsass in particular, was enormous, leading to the embrace of Postmodernist design around the world, and with particular force in the United States, Europe and Japan. Like Art Deco, in an era of instant communication it seemed to convey the dynamism and variety of modern times, with a creative freedom that could embrace Hollywood, science fiction, found objects, ancient civilizations, spiritualism, literature, art, humour and kitsch in a way that Modernism did not.

Postmodernism and politics

In the 1980s, new computer technologies helped to enable speedy prototyping and small-batch furniture production, increasing opportunities for experimentation and customization for both companies and designers. Small brands and galleries handled much of the production and distribution of Postmodernist design, aiming at collectors rather than consumers. The greatest market penetration was achieved by the homewares of upmarket Italian brand Alessi, exemplified by the exuberant kettles created by German designer Richard Sapper and American architects Michael Graves and Frank Gehry. Even so, there was some trickle down to mass markets, from the vibrancy of Swatch watches and Dyson vacuum cleaners, to retro-effect Japanese electronics and gimmicky desk accessories that replicated the style on the cheap. Edgier, allusive graphics also became prevalent in avant-garde magazines and music videos.

As the global economy boomed in the 1980s, Postmodernism came to symbolize individualism, luxury and selfishness. Perhaps it was inevitable that the iconoclastic appeal of its radical aesthetics – vivid colours, glossy surfaces and exaggerated forms – would ebb away, particularly as recession struck in the early 1990s. Faced with its apparent superficiality, consumerist ethics and, occasionally, shoddy quality, many yearned for a return to the ideals and aesthetics of Modernism, and the more restrained approach of designers such as Jasper Morrison and Naoto Fukasawa met with a receptive audience. But, alongside, expressive designers such as Philippe Starck, Tom Dixon and Ron Arad also thrived – one of Postmodernism's legacies proved to be an ongoing diversity and inclusivity in design, leaving the pursuit of both ideal form and fashionability as acceptable goals, and broadening markets from the high street to auction houses. For a long time perceived as politically and aesthetically compromised, enough time has now passed for Postmodernism's transformative qualities and positive impacts to be appreciated, and to recognize the ample space it offers for our inner lives.

The condensed idea
Less is a bore

31 Human-centred Design

Human-centred design may seem an odd proposition. Surely all design has people at its centre? There are various counters to that idea. First up, it is incumbent on most companies to turn a profit, and to produce goods that enable them to achieve this. All too frequently, that involves persuading consumers to make unnecessary purchases and product ranges are developed with this aim, rather than addressing people's real needs. Secondly, smaller segments of society with specific requirements for specialized products are often bypassed, with blanket goods for broader markets manufactured instead.

But that profit motive often goes hand in hand with designers' own predilections. Even at the peak of functionalism, in the 1950s and 1960s, much of design followed a logic that, wittingly or unwittingly, shifted humans from centre stage, focusing on the designer's conception not the user's needs. The pursuit of immaculate forms with minimal detailing produced beautiful results, but these pared-back objects tended to be far less intuitive and accessible than claimed. Similarly, in pursuit of 'universal' designs, the needs of groups positioned at either end of the bell curve got swept off the edges.

Putting people first

To avoid such propensities, the practice of human-centred design places a high priority on directly observing and empathizing with people, locating and understanding their real problems, collecting relevant data, and exploring the failings of existing solutions. Through an evolving series of prototypes, developed with close input from potential users, products are made that are both functional and enjoyable to operate. This humanistic approach involves a questioning of Modernist orthodoxies. Rather than conceptualizing and realizing products in isolation, designers are led wherever their research and their customers take them, putting aside cherished preconceptions and prejudices around uses and aesthetics.

Fresh perspectives

Perhaps tellingly, aspects of human-centred design first emerged out of engineering in the late 1950s, when John E Arnold, a professor at

Stanford University, proposed an alternative strategy for problem-solving, embracing creativity to locate and answer big questions around society's needs, rather than focusing narrowly on specific technical challenges. This new approach was given additional momentum by parallel trends from the 1960s. A new aesthetic freedom revelled in casting aside precedent; designing for comfort took increasing priority over purity of form; and, for some at least, tailoring products to children and groups with distinct needs trumped achieving a single all-encompassing solution. Finally, environmentalists began to highlight the wasteful nature of corporate behaviour. In 1971, pioneering designer and educator Victor Papanek fulminated, 'Design must become an inventive, highly creative, cross-disciplinary tool responsive to the true needs of men. It must be more research-oriented, and we must stop defiling the earth itself with poorly designed objects and structures.'

Ironically, many of these trends were also part and parcel of the emergent Postmodernist movement. Avant-garde designers started to create flamboyant products to resonate with our rich, complex lives, often deliberately rejecting the sterile pursuit of function in favour of deeper human needs. Despite this shared impetus, early human-centred design tended to be less poetic and more pragmatic in its view of people's

> It's hard to think of a vegetable peeler as radical. But I guess it was.
> Sam Farber, 2000

requirements. And, if the results were less attractive than those achieved by more dogmatic designers, they were also more effective, and more inclusive. The most cited examples are the Good Grips kitchenware range from OXO, launched in 1989, and chunky, soft toothbrushes introduced by Oral-B for children in the 1990s. Both ranges were shaped for clumsy hands, both can be visually challenging, yet both have been hugely successful. They have also given their respective brands significant cachet, and long-term profitability.

Digital expressions

Recent discussion of human-centred design has focused on digital platforms that disrupt sectors by examining the experiences and needs of potential users, and the resources and technologies available to them. Airbnb, Amazon, Spotify and Uber can all claim to have placed people at the centre of their initial product offer, and their ongoing business philosophies. Through this close engagement with users, each has successfully challenged previous assumptions and provided transformative solutions in their chosen market.

Used in a formulaic fashion by business schools and design studios, the term can often feel misleading, or even dishonest. Many successful products will be designated as 'human-centred' – their popularity would indeed suggest that a human need is being answered – even if the

The OXO Good Grips Peeler

Perhaps the ugliest product to make regular appearances on 'greatest design' lists, the Oxo Good Grips peeler comes with a rather unusual origin story. Sam Farber, having stepped back from his cookware firm, noticed that his wife Betsey, who suffered from mild arthritis, was struggling to prepare apples with a standard peeler, and promised to make her a better alternative. He hired New York–based Smart Design to help explore not just the handle, but the entirety of the peeler – its materials, dimensions and functioning. It worked with volunteers at the American Arthritis Foundation, and also with leading chefs, to understand what would surpass all their requirements, resulting in a truly inclusive product. Most striking is the ergonomic oval handle made from a soft injection-moulded plastic, Santoprene, with its flexible 'fins' to aid comfort and grip. For economy, this can be fitted on a variety of kitchen tools, and is suited to a number of different actions. Launched in 1989 at a higher price point than its competitors, the Good Grips range – 15 tools designed with functionality, clarity and accessibility in mind – was hugely successful, and now amounts to hundreds of products.

design approach played little role in their development. In addition, effectively addressing a specific set of user needs can, as in the above-mentioned digital examples, introduce significant social, economic and environmental risks in a manner that feels far from human-centred. Yet the initial proposition remains valid and important. Putting humans at the centre of the problem-solving process, from idea to product, is key to conceiving and realizing good design.

The condensed idea
Designing for people

32 National Identity

Countries expressing their identity through the production of goods – and, in particular, luxury goods – is nothing new. But, as the impacts of free trade and mass production were felt in the 19th century, design's role started to expand. Whether looking inwards to foster a sense of self, or outwards to present industrial strength and creative prowess to the world, design was transformed into a key tool for nation-building.

In these goals, the Great Exhibition, held in London's Hyde Park in 1851, proved a hugely successful pioneer, inspiring equivalent fairs at ever-increasing scales across Europe and the United States, with the French proving particularly attached to the format. The 1889 Exposition Universelle in Paris saw the inauguration of the Eiffel Tower, while its 1925 equivalent, the Exposition internationale des arts décoratifs et industriels modernes, gave birth to the Art Deco movement, cementing France's place as the leading purveyor of luxury to the world. Comparable for the United States was the 1939 New York World's Fair, heralding 'the world of tomorrow' and asserting America's primary position within it. Yet, for some countries, design has been even more important – rather than national marketing, it has acted as a means of achieving cultural and political independence.

Building nationhood

Between about 1890 and 1918, the Young Poland movement – a name coined by writer Artur Górski in his 1898 manifesto – sought to establish a distinctly Polish visual language across painting, ceramics, textiles, furniture, stained glass and graphic design. At a time when the country was partitioned, art and design were seen as critical to fomenting national identity, and to communicating it across Europe. Leading figures such as Józef Mehoffer, Karol Kłosowski and Stanisław Wyspiański – often compared to William Morris in the eclecticism of his interests and the strength of his social concerns – drew on folk art and crafts, as well as contemporary artistic movements like Expressionism, Symbolism, Art Nouveau and Pre-Raphaelitism. However, Young Poland arguably shared most DNA with the British Arts and Crafts movement, with its comparable mixture of nostalgia and modernity. Its aspirations to revive local crafts, employing their motifs and decoration, were expansive, but the village of Zakopane in the Tatra Mountains was a particular focus, its well-preserved traditions seen as a timeless expression of national character, unspoilt by cosmopolitan influences. In 1913, the short-lived Krakow Workshops shifted towards Modernism, seeking to achieve a national style through form, structure and geometry, rather than ornament, with designer Wojciech Jastrzebowski saying, 'The national character of our art was not discussed extensively, it was self-evident.' Their activities were curtailed by war, as was the entire Young Poland movement, but were to provide cultural fuel for the newly independent country in 1918 – and gain renewed relevance as a vehicle to express cultural autonomy during the Soviet dominance following World War II.

Making waves

Design as a means of building national identity – and export revenues – is epitomized by Finland's achievements after its independence in 1917. Drawing on close relationships between industry and craft, the young country made an immediate impact with the bentwood furniture of Alvar and Aino Aalto in the 1930s, as well as the pair's plywood-clad pavilion at the 1939 New York World's Fair, both suggestive of a humane alternative to the chromed rigour of continental Modernism. Yet it was the Milan Triennale – the centre of international design – that established Finland as an unlikely design superpower in 1951. Its display of lighting, textiles and, in particular, glassware was met with a rapturous reception, conveyed in both awards and press coverage that praised the sculptural organic forms and material honesty, with a wooden platter by the display's curator, Tapio Wirkkala, named as 'the most beautiful object in the world' by the US magazine *House Beautiful*. Aided by savvy campaigning, commercial partnerships and government investment, 'the miracle of Milan' was repeated over the next two decades – Finnish designs won one quarter of all prizes at the 1957 Triennale – turning designers such as Wirkkala and Timo Sarpaneva into national celebrities. Finland was revealed as a self-confident, progressive and distinctly Western country, despite its frontline position during the Cold War, with high design standards embedded across its industrial production. By the 1970s, Finland's Modernism began to seem a little austere, especially as pop culture infiltrated everyday life, yet the sustained success of companies such as Marimekko – whose dresses were favoured by US First Lady Jackie Kennedy in the 1960s – Arabia, Iittala and Artek ensures that design remains a major contributor to Finland's economy, and its national mythologies, today.

Reshaping perceptions

Finland was not alone in harnessing design in the post-war era. After making its own splash at the 1939 New York World's Fair, Brazil's 'golden years' saw the founding of the São Paulo Biennial in 1951 and the construction of a new capital, Brasilia, from 1956. Bolstered by relative stability under President Juscelino Kubitschek, a brief yet vital opportunity emerged for national re-evaluation and design experimentation, one seized with intense creativity by Sergio Rodrigues, Oscar Niemeyer, Lina Bo Bardi and others.

Perhaps the most effective single statement of design's potential to shape national identity, however, was the 1964 Olympic Games held in Tokyo, which rehabilitated Japan's reputation less than 20 years after World War II. The city underwent extensive modernization to ready its infrastructure for the Games, most famously the inauguration of the Shinkansen – the bullet train between Tokyo and Osaka – just days before the opening ceremony. Enormous energy was expended on design, spearheaded by Yusaku Kamekura, who had a hand in everything from posters to uniforms, and was responsible for the iconic logo – a red circle on a white background hovering above five interlocked golden rings, with 'Tokyo 1964' rendered in a striking sans-serif typeface. It was the first Games with a comprehensive identity system, the first to embrace Modernism, and the first with co-ordinated pictograms, designed by Yoshito Yamashita to allow for text-free navigation of the site. Presenting Japan as a modern nation, imbued with cutting-edge manufacturing and technology, the Games brought new confidence to the host nation while resetting international perceptions. But it was not without self-reflection. The Olympic cauldron was lit by 19-year-old Yoshinori Sakai, born in Hiroshima on 6 August 1945, the day the first atomic bomb was dropped.

Shifting identities

Promoting national images through design remained a significant activity in the 1990s, from the 1992 Barcelona Olympics, to the flowering of Dutch design, including Gijs Bakker's Droog Design and Rem Koolhaas' Office for Metropolitan Architecture, matched by the UK's emergence as a design force. But today, in the multi-voiced age of social media, it is harder to maintain these unified narratives. And perhaps that is no bad thing, suggestive of a productive anarchy and welcome pluralism in both nation-building and design, bringing a diversity of possibilities rather than imposing universal solutions.

The condensed idea
Designing a national image

33 Democratic Design

'**D**emocratic Design' is a somewhat equivocal concept, claimed as virtually its own by a certain well-known Swedish furniture retailer in the 1990s. But its history, and indeed its meaning, is rather more complex. Today, the term is generally used to indicate an ambition that well-designed objects will be accessible to the majority of people at a sensible price point. When used about urban planning, there is a presumption that the design process itself will be democratic – that communities can provide feedback that influences the final design – even if the reality proves less straightforward. But just how did the idea of democratic design become quite so synonymous with one global furniture and furnishings store?

Building an idea

Founded by Ingvar Kamprad in Sweden in 1943, IKEA initially sold small items such as pens and wallets before expanding into furniture, relying on high turnover and direct delivery from the factory to keep prices competitive. In the early 1950s, the company started to sell its first flatpack range, which allowed for even lower production and transportation costs, and a virtual end to the problem of damage in transit. It was the spur for IKEA's international growth, so that today there are over 450 stores in more than 60 countries, trading on a reputation for inexpensive, well-designed furniture for all. Or, as the company has described it since the Milan Furniture Fair of 1995, 'democratic design'.

IKEA claims that this concept has been key to its evolution from market disruptor to global behemoth. Distilling it down to five criteria – function, form, quality, sustainability and low price – the company maintains that a balance between all five is required for a design to be considered truly democratic. This ambition has found, perhaps, no finer expression than the much-loved BILLY bookcase, designed by Gillis Lundgren and launched in 1979. Constructed principally from particle board, and with adjustable shelves, the bookcase has proved timeless in its

> **To create a better everyday life for the many people.**
> Ingvar Kamprad

simplicity and spectacular adaptability. Hitting a sweet spot amid those five criteria, it has sold close to 150 million units to date, with no sign of slowing.

Mixed intentions

Yet the concept, if not the label, of democratic design long predates IKEA. Judged on the basis of accessibility, affordability and functionality, the advance of mechanization in the 19th century had a transformative impact, making textiles, glassware, tableware and more available in far greater quantities to new markets. Most early mass-produced items were viewed with scorn by critics, but the advent of solid bentwood furniture, invented by German-born Michael Thonet in the 1850s, indicated that mass production and design quality could be united. In particular, Chair No. 14 – a café chair consisting of just six wooden components held together by screws – sold in its millions, transported around the world disassembled, with 36 chairs slotting into a single crate. In the 1920s, it was admired by the incipient Modernist movement for its light, simple, standardized construction, Charles-Édouard Jeanneret, known as Le Corbusier, stating, 'Never was a better and more elegant design and a more precisely crafted and practical item created.'

Tensions between mass production, popular appeal and 'good design' are nothing new. In Britain, William Morris argued in the 1880s for the importance of 'necessary work-a-day furniture', proposing that it should be 'both well made and well proportioned, but simple to the last degree; nay, if it were rough I should like it the better, not the worse'. Yet his opposition to industrial production and the division of labour made this 'good citizen's furniture' unaffordable for most households. Even so, his philosophies had a wide influence. In Sweden, the pioneering writer Ellen Key championed 'worker's furniture', stating in her seminal *Beauty for All* (1899) that, if introduced into the home, beautiful objects – practical, natural and expressing both their purposes and the souls of their creators – would lead to a better life, and a better society.

Increasingly, forging a relationship between art and industry was seen as key to ensuring that mass-produced objects met acceptable standards of quality and taste. In his 1919 work *Better Things for Everyday Life*, the Swedish art historian and critic Gregor Paulsson argued that art belonged to everyone, and that introducing it to factories would bring aesthetic, economic and social benefits. This belief was an expression of progressive social ideals in Sweden that would later be expressed at IKEA, and that were shared by many Modernist architects and designers in the wake of World War I. Improving people's lives through affordable everyday items chimed with the development of Existenzminimum apartments across many European cities in the 1920s. Rapidly built, functional, hygienic and

Keeping a lid on it

If IKEA has cornered the modern claim on democratic design, it may be argued that Tupperware was scaling up the concept even earlier. Founded by chemist Earl Tupper in 1942, his Tupper Corporation experimented with injection-moulded polyethylene for homewares, gaining a patent for the 'Tupper Seal' five years later. The resulting leak-proof containers, with their airtight double seal, proved slow to catch on, but eventually became practical and cultural staples, found in the cupboards of mid-century American homes of all classes. The firm's early business model, based on social networking at parties, was distinctly egalitarian too, helping women generate an income and facilitating their entrance into the workforce. Subsequent evidence suggests that some of this democratization was at least a little illusory – very few selling agents rose above the lowest level of cash-generation – but Tupperware's products remain an example of quality utilitarian items available to virtually all.

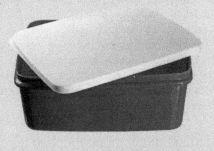

compact – exemplified by the New Frankfurt housing programme that constructed 12,000 apartments in five years from 1925 (many with a Frankfurt Kitchen, see page 30) – they were intended to provide a minimum acceptable standard of living at a time of widespread poverty and severe housing shortages.

For better and worse

Democratic design is not without its critics. Achieving cost-efficient designs with broad appeal encourages a reduction in risk-taking, resulting in conservative products rather than innovative ones. Similarly, in its pursuit of universal application and appeal, democratic design can paradoxically fail to be inclusive, ignoring disability, old age, gender differences or the needs of marginalized communities. Finally, it can overlook one of design's most important roles – the expression of individuality – proposing one single solution rather than embracing plurality. But for all that, there is much to admire in that goal of providing the greatest number of people with good-quality products at affordable prices, whether adjustable bookshelves, efficient household appliances, or perhaps even the life-altering internet.

The condensed idea
Good design for everyone

34 Luxury

The relationship between design and luxury is awkward. Once upon a time, design was a utopian discipline, dedicated to the ideal of a just, equitable society. In the 1920s and 1930s, totally new designs were conceived with a view to mass production, intended as affordable, universal products that would be available to all, and improve the lives of all. That vision, and the extraordinary designs that resulted, bestowed an elevated status – an aura of nobility and insight – that the discipline has never lost, and that was only enhanced by its emergence as a respected profession in the 1950s. To end up as a byword for luxury, for exclusivity and expense, feels unfortunate. Today when 'designer sunglasses' are mentioned, large price tags and glossy adverts come to mind, or knock-offs falling off the backs of lorries. Design has come a long way.

What is luxury?

The idea of luxury is elastic and subjective, yet has enormous power, driving an industry worth hundreds of billions of dollars annually. Finding a one-size-fits-all definition is impossible, but aspirations to aesthetic excellence, and an associated exclusivity, are crucial to justify high prices, quite apart from a deluxe appearance, handcrafting or extra features. To be overly pious about luxury is a mistake. Introducing beauty into one's life, and seeking personal and public self-affirmation, are entirely legitimate goals. At certain moments in the past, however, luxury has been associated with vanity and self-indulgence, even regarded as a sin. It remains condemned by some communities today, attacked for greed, selfishness or ostentation. In whatever era such criticisms have been made, they have often been honoured more in the breach than the observation – forsaking luxury can be a challenge.

Changing priorities

Definitions of luxury have evolved over time. In the West, goods that were once considered the preserve of an elite, from extensive wardrobes, to decent homes, to last year's digital devices stuffed in a drawer, are now commonplace. Delving into the past, very different materials and production methods were available, and soap, cinnamon and purple dye (see box) were seen as luxurious. Associating scarcity with luxury does, at least, have some validity. Today, that scarcity is artificial – a brand's logo or a celebrity's involvement (usually both) can do the job, or the exclusivity of a limited edition, or merely an inflated price. Through these tactics, a standard trainer or handbag becomes a collector's item, tagged as 'designer' to communicate prestige, worn in public as a symbol of wealth and taste, or left in a box for personal satisfaction – unless undermined by the regrettable behaviour of said celebrity.

This isn't just a recent phenomenon driven by the rise of consumerism. Many serious-minded, respected, innovative figures from the golden age of Modernism in the mid-20th century worked almost exclusively for brands operating at the top end of the market.

Despite the idealism of the Bauhaus, and its advocacy of mass production, just four of Mies van der Rohe's Barcelona chairs were produced in 1929 as a 'monumental object' for the German pavilion at the Barcelona International Exposition. More tellingly, in 1953 Mies granted production rights to the upmarket American manufacturer Knoll, which had opened its new Madison Avenue showroom just two years earlier and counted the Rockefeller family as regular clients. The company attached a dramatic price tag to the iconic chair, and remain its primary producers to this day. The innovative designers Charles and Ray Eames – prophets of a relaxed modern lifestyle – had a similarly profitable relationship with another American manufacturer, Herman Miller. Such close relationships have become less common, with designers working across brands as 'guns for hire', but their imprimatur remains much sought-after by companies, guaranteeing a prestige and price that unlicensed versions lack – and often greater quality too. Mies, for instance, oversaw Knoll's production until his death in 1969. To preserve this luxury status, an expensive lawsuit is always lurking around the corner for companies producing knock-offs.

> Some people think luxury is the opposite of poverty. It is not. It is the opposite of vulgarity.
>
> Coco Chanel

Luxury today

From some perspectives, luxury is now at an interesting juncture. For one thing, ostentatious and unnecessary consumption is at odds with environmental concerns, whether that involves the flaunting of precious materials and elaborate ornament, ceaseless air travel around chic destinations, or the pursuit of perfect minimalist lifestyles that require resources of space and labour unaffordable for the vast majority. Movements such as the Buy Nothing Project, with its advice to 'share more, spend less', or Degrowth, attacking capitalism's endless pursuit of productivity, are becoming more persuasive than the luxury market's 'design with a conscience' alternative. In addition, the balance between exclusivity and market share is proving harder to maintain. Luxury brands are now attracting wide swathes of consumers that could be seen as undermining their precious cachet. Affordable ranges risk further brand dilution; increasingly and unjustifiably expensive ones risk making companies, products and purchasers all appear ridiculous, while whittling away market share.

But, as stated, luxury remains a legitimate human goal. It is just up to each individual where they find the beauty, satisfaction, affirmation and happiness they seek. Although, if the well-being industry has its way, you'll need to be wearing the right yoga pants at the time.

The condensed idea
Finding luxury wherever you choose

35 Design Thinking

There are many competing definitions of design thinking, most proposed by consultancies or academics touting for business. The concept has roots in the 1960s, when industrial design established itself as fundamental to product delivery and company success, and was increasingly tackling our interactions with machines and technology. Focus, and the self-interest of a new breed of professional design organizations, turned to defining the skills and processes that lay behind this powerful tool, so important to the realization of everything from consumer goods to the space programme.

The rational designer

Companies began to analyse design as a science as much as an art, considering it alongside – and possibly even above – other 'scientific' aspects of company activity such as 'human factors engineering', which tackled human interactions with machines, systems and workspaces, and 'management science', which focused on company structures and decision-making. They sought an underlying methodology that could be applied to product development, or even transferred to the running of companies, employing the tactics of industrial design: collecting data around existing or attainable materials, resources and technologies, and about the requirements of users, markets and environments. The intention was to monitor structures and costs while developing, prototyping and delivering solutions, drawing expertise from multiple disciplines. Somewhere within this process, the generation of ideas would be scattered.

Academic momentum gathered behind this approach, sometimes called the 'design methods movement', given impetus by the work of systems scientist Christopher Alexander at the University of California, Berkeley, who argued for design as a universal tool with diverse applications. *Notes on the Synthesis of Form*, which he published in 1964, explored how design can act to solve complex problems, and proposed a systematic method that could be employed in a linear fashion, foregrounding logic rather than intuition. Nobel Prize-winner Herbert Simon took this further, proposing a science of design – 'a body of intellectually tough, analytic, partly formalizable, partly empirical, teachable doctrine about the design process' – that could even be transformed into a problem-solving computer program, acting as a form of artificial intelligence.

Such presumptions around design's nature – and its benefits – began to be questioned from the late 1960s, along with wider notions of social and scientific progress in which the discipline was so heavily invested. For design theorist Horst Rittel, to address deep-rooted, open-ended 'wicked problems' in business or society with a series of simplifications and routine steps was likely to result in inadequate answers, yet these were problems in which 'the designer had no right to be wrong', with ethical implications and long-term impacts if tackled incorrectly. Rittel and others such as Bruce Archer also pointed to inherent challenges around defining problems in the first place, and choosing sources of information and desired solutions, which risked embedding issues rather than solving them.

> Everyone designs who devises courses of action aimed at changing existing situations into preferred ones.
> Herbert Simon, 1969

From guru to suit

If design's enmeshing within corporate and scientific structures led to a backlash, as evidenced by criticisms from social designer Victor Papanek, the rehabilitation was rapid, aided by the emergence of the designer as a guru figure in both alternative culture and the digital revolution. The lure of the word 'design' proved just too powerful for it to be sidelined for long, even if ambiguity, participation and intuition were now given greater prominence. In 1986, British academic Nigel Cross explored the unique nature of the designer's method and mindset in *Designerly Ways of Knowing*, looking at the strategies used by designers to generate ideas and solutions, while the following year, architect Peter Rowe published *Design Thinking* – the first book of this title – seeking commonalities between different ways of evolving forms and solving problems in architecture and urban planning.

San Francisco-based company IDEO, founded in 1991 but with roots in traditional industrial design in the 1970s, successfully introduced this updated design thinking to the corporate sphere. It developed a six-step methodology to problem-solving, with a greater

Despite the shift away from formalized steps and towards greater flexiblity, the 'hexagon diagram' remains one of the major tools in design thinking, incorporating five phases: 'Empathize', 'Define', 'Ideate', 'Prototype' and 'Test'. It first emerged from the d.school at Stanford University, established in 2004 as a leading centre for design thinking with involvement from IDEO. The process is intended to be non-linear and iterative, avoiding charges of rigidity, although the disappearance of any delivery stage has led to criticism that the significant challenges of implementation in real life – the costs, disruptions, resistance – remain ones that design tends to duck.

DESIGN THINKING PROCESS

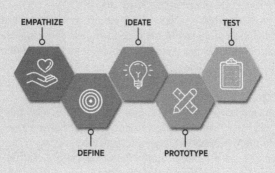

focus on empathy, reflection, creativity and innovation than the 1960s approach. Information is gathered by observing end users; ideas are generated, with a concern for needs; rapid improvisational prototyping follows; feedback is gathered; versions are iterated; then implementation takes place. This people-centred process is intended to be used by anyone – not just designers – in order to improve both lives and balance sheets, tackling anything from robotics, to healthcare, to homelessness.

By the 2000s, design thinking was flourishing in universities and business schools as both practice and buzz phrase, evolving into a form of consultancy for corporations and public institutions. In tandem with the expansion of 'service design', in which companies sought to shape their entire relationship with consumers, designers were now being hired to bring design's qualities to bear on delivering specific projects or reshaping wider structures and processes. This 'designer as consultant' approach is not without its critics, who suggest that superficial or ephemeral solutions may result, ignoring longer-term ethical and social issues. For many, 'design thinking' is little more than management consultancy rebranded with a trendier, and more lucrative, name.

The debate is ongoing, but design thinking's focus on collaboration is perhaps its key strength, bringing together skill sets and knowledge across disciplines and departments to arrive at fresh ideas, and embedding cultures and networks of innovation throughout organizations, whether private firms or housing projects. Rather than unique possessors of universal problem-solving magic, the designer, and design itself, become pragmatic facilitators of a process, one in which all participants are co-designers.

The condensed idea
Designing solutions for business

36 Design for Play

Design has many purposes, among them problem-solving, artistic expression and financial gain. Another purpose is to mould tastes or behaviours. A powerful example of the latter – and one that brings with it a special responsibility – is designing for children. Toys provide some of a child's earliest and most important interactions with the world, and are wrapped up in emotional, educational and physical growth, shaping both their everyday and future lives.

The key to creativity

From the 18th century, childhood and education came to be seen as valid experiences in themselves, not merely preparation for adulthood – experiences that should involve learning through play and the enjoyment of nature. Alongside the ever-increasing production of toy soldiers, trains, tea sets and dolls, new educational toys were introduced for the purpose of 'open-ended play', free of fixed outcomes, leaving children free to gain valuable skills and wider insights. Most famous are the six 'gifts', from yarn balls to simple wooden blocks, devised by Friedrich Froebel, the founder of the kindergarten movement, in the 1830s. These were intended to help children make judgements about the relationships between things, helping them understand the unity of the natural world, and were cited as inspiration by American architects Frank Lloyd Wright and Buckminster Fuller. Later, in a commercialized form and often with a male focus, numerous construction toys arrived, offering their own take on these educational goals, such as Germany's Anchor Blocks, introduced in 1880, or Britain's Meccano, available from 1898.

That division between playthings recreating the world in miniature – the toy soldiers and baby dolls – and the abstract toys intended to encourage experimentation and imagination has remained a constant theme in progressive circles, with eloquent writers lining up to attack the former. German philosopher Walter Benjamin wrote in 1928 that 'the more appealing toys are, in the ordinary sense of the term, the further they are from genuine playthings; the more they are based on imitation, the further away they lead us from real, living play'. Thirty years later, French critic Roland Barthes decried such toys as generating 'a microcosm of the adult world', in which 'the child does not invent the world, he uses it: there are, prepared for him, actions without adventure, without wonder, without joy'. Equipped with the 'merest set of blocks', however, the child 'creates forms that walk, that roll; he creates life, not property'.

The Modernist toy

That toys should be simple forms with multiple applications – ones that acted as systems rather than objects – chimed perfectly with Modernist beliefs around fostering creativity, and in particular with the Bauhaus's famous preliminary course, which focused on colour, shape, composition and materials. In the 1920s, student Alma Siedhoff-Buscher designed groups of striking building blocks in bright colours, some combining simple geometric forms to teach balance and movement, some a little more refined, capable of creating ships, bridges and landscapes. Italian artists Giacomo Balla and Fortunato Depero were a little more extravagant in their objectives, stating that their futurist 'assemblages' would unlock children's imagination, elasticity and sensitivity, making them laugh out loud, but also keeping adults 'young, agile, jubilant, spontaneous, ready for anything, untiring, instinctive and intuitive'.

The most famous manifestation of this Modernist belief in the power of play was The Toy – a grandiose title suggesting the definitive plaything had been designed – launched by Charles and Ray Eames, the golden couple of American industrial design, in 1951. This ingenious construction kit of colourful triangles and squares joined by pipe cleaners and dowels was capable of creating

> **Toys are not really for children, toys are really for adults – especially grandparents.**
> Charles Eames, 1973

tunnels, tents and theatres. Charles proclaimed on the occasion: 'Toys are really not as innocent as they look. Toys and games are the preludes to serious ideas.' The kit remained in production for just eight years. It turned out that the most successful Modernist plaything was not really a toy, but a puzzle. The Rubik's Cube was created during workshops held by architect Ernö Rubik at the Budapest Academy of Applied Arts in 1974, and is believed to be the best-selling single toy in the world.

Unlocking profits

For Modernist ideals to really conquer the toy world, commercial acumen was required. LEGO – an abbreviation of the Danish phrase *leg godt* (play well) – was founded in 1932 by Ole Kirk Kristiansen. Having recently launched a 'LEGO System of Play', with a town plan that let children build their own cities with colourful plastic blocks, the famous stud-and-tube system of interlocking bricks ('for girls, for boys') was introduced in 1958. Ole's son, Christian, pronounced: 'Our idea has been to create a toy that prepares the child for life – appealing to their imagination and developing the creative urge and joy of creation that are the driving forces in every human being.' It would seem to work – around 70 billion elements are now sold every year.

But 'elements' is an important word. Under threat from the smiling figures and perfectly conceived worlds of up-and-coming German rival Playmobil, in the 1970s Lego shifted its focus away from those colourful construction blocks, introducing miniature figures and specialized bricks with strict instruction manuals for its new town, space and castle themes. The commercial results were impressive, even if the market was largely male. Accelerated by the success of *Star Wars* action figures, the company's Modernist ideals around non-prescriptive play had fallen prey to financial imperatives, but also to

Marketing takes over

The unprecedented success of *Star Wars* action figures, first released in 1978, underlined the importance of licensing and tie-ins for toy manufacturers. Aided by advertising deregulation in the 1980s, the worlds of children's entertainment and marketing merged into one with 'Program-Length Commercials', or PLCs. Toy companies sponsored cartoon series featuring their own products, for instance *He Man*, *My Little Pony* and *Teenage Mutant Ninja Turtles*, shifting huge quantities of figurines as a result. It turned out that all this cheap plastic granted children access to rich imaginative worlds and strong characters – attractions that carried rather more weight than high-quality design.

children's love of engaging scenarios and strong stories. LEGO's tie-ups with the Star Wars and Harry Potter franchises would follow, as would its own inventive movies.

Letting go

The ambition of Modernist designers to create abstract toys to spark children's creativity and curiosity was an optimistic one. As with much of the Modernist project, it sprang from a belief that a better society could be fashioned, and better citizens to live in it. Yet their experimental toys now find their home largely in coffee-table books and design stores, purchased by parents and godparents, acting as expensive ornaments for adults. It turns out that children are highly skilled in wriggling away from whatever adults feel is best for them – a feeling wrapped up in nostalgia or notions of lost innocence – and towards *Star Wars* or Super Mario.

Whether the freedom of children to shape their own play or protecting them from rampant consumerism should take precedence – and which approach delivers the best educational results – is still being disputed. The reality certainly doesn't have to be binary, but denying children agency in that choice and enforcing freeform play seems both paradoxical and unsustainable.

The condensed idea
Let the children play

37 Green Design

As the environmental movement gathered force in the 1960s, a tentative reassessment of design's place in the world began. Given the growing awareness of humankind's impact on nature, architects and designers began to explore practices that minimized, or at least significantly reduced, environmental damage. Such contemplative texts as Aldo Leopold's *A Sand County Almanac* (1949) paved the way, along with some more polemical ones like Fairfield Osborn's *Our Plundered Planet* (1948), with its unfortunate yet unexceptional fixation on population growth. But the book that really caught the American public's attention was *Silent Spring* (1962) by conservationist Rachel Carson, a powerful warning against 'the reckless and irresponsible poisoning of the world' resulting from the overuse of pesticides, and by implication an indictment of the chemical industry.

Just nine years later, *Design for the Real World* by the Austrian-born designer Victor Papanek was published. In contrast to the analytical, if occasionally lyrical, *Silent Spring*, this was a polemical attack on industrial design as greedy, shortsighted and destructive, stating – to take one example among many – that 'by creating a whole new species of permanent garbage to clutter up the landscape, and by choosing materials and processes that pollute the air we breathe, designers have become a dangerous breed'. Papanek argued that design should aspire to become an agent for positive change and, by this point, some within academia and industry were starting to listen. There was a growing acceptance that design came with specific responsibilities, in view of its enabling role in consumerism and its primary place in product development. Given such influence over industry, designers could not avoid some degree of culpability for its social and ecological impacts.

Green shoots

One upshot was the establishment of a multitude of heavyweight environmental groups in the late 1960s and early 1970s. Some were relatively conventional campaigning organizations, such as Friends of the Earth; others took a more activist stance, such as Greenpeace.

There were also new government bodies concerned with ecology, such as the United States' Environmental Protection Agency, and intra-governmental ones, for instance the United Nations Environment Programme. All played an important role in raising awareness, providing momentum and, equally importantly, getting legislation on the statute book, with the United States' Clean Water Act passed in 1972. Dramatic increases in oil prices in the early 1970s provided added urgency, highlighting manufacturers' over-reliance on fossil fuels as a source of both energy and plastics. Such disasters as the devastating chemical spill at Bhopal, India, in 1984 also revealed the environmental degradation and human suffering that global companies were leaving in their wake.

Accelerated by public concern, the installation of technologies such as solar panels grew during the 1970s, as did the availability of recyclable products and packaging, and the introduction of recycling programmes. A new focus on energy efficiency led to improvements in home insulation and a shift towards smaller cars and lower-energy appliances. Yet, half a century later, these conversations, and these shifts, are still a work in progress. At certain moments, public or political pressure on companies has resulted in high-profile environmental initiatives, with ambitious Green projects launched, whether from noble intentions, or fear of reputational damage, or both. 'Sustainable design' also emerged as a related discipline, with a greater focus on holistic approaches that take social and economic factors into account. Overall, there has been real change, but in many ways, convenience and profitability have ensured that such traditional industry practices as planned obsolescence, oil dependence and disposable products remain the default mindset. Plastic production continues to rise, while the lightly policed plethora of eco-friendly badges invites confusion and cynicism about their efficacy and purpose.

Designing change

The shifting of narratives, and practices, is a long, slow undertaking. With policy decisions made at corporate and governmental level, designers have surprisingly little influence over the direction of travel. Green design projects tend to be more educational than transformational, generating products that propose low-tech alternatives or high-tech solutions to ecological challenges, and rarely achieve mass production or distribution. In these projects, often commissioned by high-end companies or as one-off ranges, common materials are reinvented as alluring ones, old products and waste are repurposed, recycled, and biodegradable materials foregrounded, and energy-efficient or natural solutions proposed. The results are admirable, but more aesthetic than effective – like the abundance of eco-friendly badges, they often act as a marketing tactic rather than a strategy for change.

Certification programmes are playing an important role in validating green claims, some run by global nonprofits such as the Forest Stewardship Council, promoting responsible management of the world's forests, some by smaller organizations such as the German Passivhaus Institut, mandating rates of energy consumption in housing. But there is no escaping the fact that governmental and intergovernmental legislation remains the essential tool for turning all these conversations into reality.

Rethinking priorities

During the early 2000s, the longstanding slogan of the Green movement, 'reduce, reuse, recycle', came under scrutiny. Through the lens of 'whole life-cycle assessments' – looking at the entirety of a product's impact from material extraction to final disposal – the focus on recycling in particular seemed problematic. Intensive in labour and energy use, the carbon benefits can be disappointing, while the declining quality of recycled materials is an unavoidable reality. In effect, when it comes to tackling the challenge of finite resources, recycling is a delaying tactic rather than a solution, with repair, reuse and durability providing important, if not complete, answers. Upcycling of products – not as a source of junkshop coffee tables, but as an industrial process, creating new materials, products or even nutrients – is increasingly seen as key, leading to the current focus on the circular economy and a 'cradle to cradle' approach.

> In every outthrust headland, in every curving beach, in every grain of sand there is the story of the earth.
> Rachel Carson, 1958

Recycling, and in particular plastic recycling, may have flaws, often acting more as a fig leaf than a solution, but that does not make it futile. It increases the life of materials and lessens production of new plastics. It also gains us time to find uses for the waste we have already produced, and to develop urgently needed technologies, and even lifestyles, for the future. In some ways, the same goes for Green design as a whole. Despite not providing real answers, it has played a key role in an ongoing process of learning, awareness and improvement – but it's time to move on.

The condensed idea
Designing for nature

38 Digital Design

Not so long ago, an entry on digital design in a compendium such as this would carry with it a frisson of excitement, hinting at a multitude of uncharted possibilities. As the discipline has become universal, that frisson has diminished, but the possibilities remain. In the 1980s, a major medium for explorations in digital design would have been paper. For graphic designers, whether creating posters, packaging, books or magazines, technology opened innumerable doors, with access to digital typefaces and imagery increasing rapidly, pushing aside analogue alternatives. And, as new software such as MacPaint and, eventually, Adobe Photoshop arrived, manipulation, collaging, distortion and layering of elements became feasible, to unprecedented effect.

One of the most exciting pioneers was April Greiman. By the early 1980s, the New York–based designer had moved far from her training in the rigours of the International Style, exploring the uncharted capabilities of the Apple Macintosh, but also working with – even celebrating – its limitations. With its expressive and occasionally unsettling aesthetic, Greiman's work made creative use of digital technologies and, in doing so, offered an enticing vision in which graphic design moved away from specific functions within publishing, and towards an unprecedented freedom. Others followed, such as David Carson, with the alluring chaos of his 'grunge typography', and Neville Brody, shifting from earlier New Romantic album covers to award-winningly subversive digital typefaces.

> It's not graphic design anymore. We just don't have a new name for it yet.
> April Greiman, 1984

Going virtual

Gaming was also an important medium for the development of digital design, moving from 1960s pioneers such as *Spacewar!*, via early arcade games and the arrival of the personal computer in the 1970s, and eventually to the immersive, multiplayer environments with complex story lines and million-strong followings we know today. For the traditional design community, however, the launch of the World

Wide Web in 1989 – and, two years later, the first website – was more immediately pertinent. This new arena of information provision related directly to the most significant part of the graphic designer's skillset – and those skills were seemingly transferable. It took a while for mainstream websites to join the initial burst of science and computing forums, with Bloomberg an early adopter in 1993, followed swiftly by the BBC, *The Economist*, *The Simpsons* and a Santa Cruz pizza-ordering service. Digital design no longer meant trying out new features on Adobe Photoshop, but exploring an entirely new and transformative medium.

At first, much graphic design on the web involved the replication of existing physical formats, with long, narrow columns of diminutive text that paid little attention to accessibility, but were quick to download with dial-up connections. It took a while, but as technology improved and audiences grew, it became clear that websites had significant advantages print didn't. One of those – the ability to track user behaviour – gave unprecedented insights into the performance of content, impacting on the nature and layout of the material provided, along with the design of the site as a whole. Even more, it gave detailed feedback on the performance of adverts – *Wired* magazine is cited as being the first to get in on the market in 1994 – gradually eroding the precedence given to providing information. Instead, a complex and muddy list of priorities emerged, with the key function of websites and online graphic design changing from serving the needs of readers to serving the needs of those footing the bill – the advertisers. And somewhere along the line, graphic design's aspirations to mix clear communication with attractive, if unobtrusive, aesthetics started slipping down the hierarchy. Even enjoyably chaotic attempts to create immersive environments – such as batmanforever.com, which, in 1995, plunged the fan into the world of Gotham City – were pushed aside for more immediately commercial designs.

Total design

Today, digital design operates within very strict parameters. One of those is the hardware on which it is accessed, a relationship so intimate that it is increasingly difficult to separate where digital design ends and physical design begins. If the embrace of Apple's graphic user interfaces was facilitated by the success of the Macintosh (and

The rise of emoji

The greatest visual and communicatory device of digital design has been a diminutive icon known as an emoji. Used as a shorthand to denote intended meanings, objects or emotional responses, these are now a universal and ubiquitous digital language, transcending borders and cultures. Emojis emerged from 'emoticons', letters, numbers and punctuation marks employed to mimic things, often facial expressions. In circulation as 'typographical art' as early the 19th century, they were given a vibrant new life by the internet. The first set of bespoke emojis – a term combining the Japanese words for picture and character – was created by Japanese designer Shigetaka Kurita in 1998 for mobile phones and pagers. Designed on a 12-by-12-pixel grid, the full set comprised an impressive total of 176 symbols, from a snowman to a broken heart. Today, there are at least 20 times that number, and the grip of these modern-day hieroglyphs shows no signs of loosening, with an estimated 92 per cent of the global online population now using them.

vice versa), by the time of the iPhone this symbiosis was complete – all design had to work within the confines of this digital portal, and its operating systems. Today, this closed ecosystem has resulted in applications adopting a series of formulaic graphic devices and approaches to navigation, most of which are now more or less compulsory. To diverge is to depart from 'intuitive' norms, and so risk losing users frustrated by encountering the unexpected. Many of these norms have been established via familiarity rather than intuition, and are often the result of small, improvisational steps, each building on the next, rather than a more cohesive vision. In addition, the definition of user is one driven by commercial interests, as are the designs of interfaces. With the advance of artificial intelligence, the reach, precision and impact of these definitions and designs are only likely to grow.

If the frisson of excitement around digital design has ebbed away, it certainly retains the potential to surprise, and perhaps even overturn our expectations. Alternatively, the opportunity remains to return to paper, pick up a copy of *Ray Gun* or *Wired*, and discover what creative freedom looks like.

The condensed idea
New possibilities, new challenges

39 Service Design

Despite a rather unglamorous name, service design is a rapidly expanding and increasingly important field in the management of organizations, one that seeks to create processes that work for all stakeholders throughout the delivery of a service. Whether transport, insurance, healthcare or haircuts, every stage in the execution and reception of that service is carefully planned and organized, looking at the people, processes and systems involved in a holistic fashion, but with a particular focus on the 'customer journey' – identifying the 'touchpoints' at which the user and the service meet, some of them tangible, some less so, and seeking to understand and optimize the nature of that encounter.

Robust service design needs to be comprehensive, working for all parties and prepared for all eventualities, including the unpredictability of a spontaneous exchange. That could be the customer complaining of a damaged product, or the account holder concerned about an unexpected transaction. The strength of a company's reputation and its future success – as a provider of luxury automobiles or banking services – relies on its ability to provide a high-quality, user-friendly service throughout. And, as the intermeshing of the physical and the digital continues, the number and complexity of those touchpoints between company and consumer, and thus the significance of service design as an approach, will only continue to grow, particularly as data gathering, feedback and artificial intelligence are fully integrated into the process.

From product to service

There has always been an overlap between products and services – when we go to, say, a restaurant, which one is on offer? But in the modern world, the distinction between the two is becoming even more blurred. With technologies such as music streaming, much of the product on offer has become wrapped up within the service. A comprehensive selection of music and sound quality are certainly important when choosing a preferred platform, but so are ease of access and navigation, provision of storage, download speeds, cross-device synchronization and – perhaps most important, bar the price

– the success of the algorithms that offer bespoke personal playlists along the way. As coffee shops have always known, the core product is not necessarily top of the list when it comes to keeping customers loyal – it is only one element in a complete and coherent experience being offered to the consumer.

> When you have two coffee shops right next to each other, selling the exact same coffee at the exact same price, service design is what makes you walk into the one and not the other, come back often and tell your friends about it.
>
> Marc Fonteijn, 31 Volts, Utrecht

Straight speaking

The coining of the term 'service design' in 1982, and a good deal of its associated early theoretical work, is credited to marketing consultant G Lynn Shostack, who noted that, at the time, 'People confuse services with products and with good manners.' She believed that this ad hoc, fragmented approach to services was highly damaging, particularly as the US transitioned to a service economy: 'Leaving services to individual talent and managing the pieces rather than the whole. . . makes a company more vulnerable and creates a service that reacts slowly to market needs and opportunities.' To help organizations get on top of the complex interactions of people, materials, infrastructure and processes, she outlined the necessity for a rigorous 'service blueprint' – in essence a complex flowchart outlining how a service is delivered by the provider and experienced by the customer – breaking that process down into sequential steps, including all interactions, variables, fail points and time frames. It also highlighted opportunities for feedback, iteration and experimentation in pursuit of increased profits. Her ideas, and approach, were rapidly embraced and extended, with the Köln International School of Design teaching it as an academic discipline from 1991, and its subsequent adoption by major consultancies such as IDEO and Liveworks.

Going global

By the turn of the 21st century, service design had become well established in private business, with sophisticated models driving companies as diverse as Starbucks and Amazon to success. The interdisciplinary and expansive nature of the discipline became evident as designers, managers, software engineers, marketeers and more became involved in its delivery, and experts in areas such as psychology and anthropology began to be called in. But an important moment came in 2002 when three Danish ministries combined to establish MindLab, one of the world's first service-design consultancies for the public sector. This new body proved successful in improving services for everyone from jobseekers to business start-ups, but also drove cross-departmental collaboration and innovative thinking across all sectors of government. Around the globe, countries have since adopted service design in the provision of their public services, a trend that segues with growing interest in the application of certain fields of psychological research to government business. In particular, behaviourism and its subcategory, 'nudge theory' – the idea that human behaviours can be influenced through 'soft' interventions – have been embraced, with 'nudge units' formed in the United Kingdom, Germany, Japan and the United States.

The McDonald's model

Although they set up their business decades before service design even had a name, the MacDonald brothers, Dick and Mac, have a good claim to being early exponents. In the 1940s, their drive-thru barbecue joint in San Bernardino, California, was doing well enough. But the brothers coolly analysed its flaws, which included an over-extensive menu and long wait times for food. They realized that most people ordered burgers and fries from the menu, along with a drink and a desert. With an eye to customer satisfaction, they scaled back their food offering and devised a food-preparation and delivery system that meant consumers could tuck into their burger within a minute of ordering. They designed a top-to-tail system regulating the entire process from buying the necessary ingredients to delivering the finished product in a welcoming setting, and kept that system under almost constant review. The McDonald's dining model might not be for everyone, but the brothers created a business that worked for its franchisees, employees and users – and for Ray Kroc, the one-time franchisee who bought the brothers out, and went on to create a global giant.

Total impact

Uber is regularly cited as an example of how service design is suited to smoothing the highly complex path of businesses that inhabit both the real world and the digital space. Despite large numbers of its diverse workforce never actually meeting, its drivers, app developers and accountants – and everyone else in between – are part of a long process that successfully delivers a multiphase customer experience, from signing up to the Uber service and providing payment details, to booking transport, to taking a journey, and on to after-service feedback and support. Just like the similarly successful Airbnb, however, this sophisticated structure has proved so effective, and so cohesive, that it has significantly disrupted existing business models and their surrounding ecosystems, with unexpected consequences for town centres and traditional businesses, and accompanying concerns around gig economies and data privacy. Now that service design has become so key to how we live our lives, there is a risk it may be too powerful for its own good. Perhaps, with all due respect to G Lynn Shostack, it may be time to start leaving services to individual talent again, and managing the pieces rather than the whole.

The condensed idea
Designing the entire journey

40 Design Art

Given that modern design sprang from the decorative arts, 'design art' might seem a superfluous term. The 'decorative' arts encompass a vast range of products that do not fall within the scope of the 'fine' arts of painting and sculpture, yet they comprehend innumerable items that merit the term 'art'. There has usually, although not always, been a divergence in the status accorded to creators working in the two fields. Said Gilani, the imperial goldsmith responsible for Shah Jahan's jewel-encrusted Peacock throne – commissioned in 1628 to celebrate the Shah's accession and the rise of the Mughal Empire – was rewarded with his own weight in gold coins when it was finally completed in 1635. But, at twice the cost of the contemporary Taj Mahal, and incorporating the Koh-i-Noor diamond later exhibited at London's Crystal Palace, this extravagant seat, and the recognition accorded to its maker, were exceptions rather than rules.

On the whole, the names and reputations of early designers, and their workshops, do not survive in this way. With effort, the artists who painted elaborate panels for Renaissance *cassoni* – marriage chests – can sometimes be discovered, but those who created the chests themselves remain anonymous. By the 18th century, the names of designers associated with major pattern books, or with royal and aristocratic patrons, do sometimes survive, for instance the fashionable English furniture designer Thomas Chippendale, or the French royal cabinet maker Jean-Henri Riesener. But it was only in the 19th century, as the decorative arts achieved wider circulation, greater commercial heft and more overt social significance, owing in large part to mass production, that the situation changed radically. In the context of growing discourse around design, figures such as William Morris or Charles Eastlake became intimately associated with specific objects, styles and philosophical positions. In many ways, their outputs and ideas were more interesting than the academic art of the time, with a greater relevance to society, and were recognized as such by contemporaries.

Useless furniture

So why, by this point, haven't we reached the era of design art? Largely because the objects themselves, however rich in meaning, were designed for use – in fact their significance was often embodied in that fact. That distinction was finally thrust aside by the Surrealists in the 1930s. Some items might display a vestige of practicality, such as the pair of Mae West sofas designed by Salvador Dalí for the West Sussex home of collector Edward James – modelled on an earlier painting by the artist, their red fabric was chosen after a hot pink was rejected by James as 'too flashy'. Other Surrealist works cast aside use entirely, for example Dalí's half-size *Venus de Milo* (1936) with

> Design is a way of discussing life. It is a way of discussing society, politics, eroticism, food and even design. At the end, it is a way of building up a possible figurative utopia or metaphor about life.
> Ettore Sottsass, 1993

functioning drawers sporting mink tufts as handles scattered across her body, relating to his fascination with the theories of Sigmund Freud. The artist himself described the sculpture as 'absolutely useless. . .and created wholly for the purpose of materializing in a fetishistic way, with maximum tangible reality, ideas and fantasies of a delirious character'.

A similar trend of artists appropriating the forms of furniture blossomed in the 1960s. Richard Artschwager's thoroughly impractical, largely solid and unconvincingly illusionistic *Table and Chair* of 1964–65 is one of a series that he explained by saying, 'These works consist of both the object and the image thereof; they are both. The first fact puts them in the realm of the useful; the second, in the realm of the useless.' One could make a list of similar artists of the era, but probably the most interesting is Donald Judd. His pared-back wooden furniture of the 1970s, initially made for his Spring Street studio, embraces use, if occasionally in mild discomfort, and Judd made a clear distinction between these objects and his art practice.

Engaging with art

Strangely, even now we haven't reached design art – perhaps one might call the above 'art design' in which artists co-opted the physical form or elements of furniture as commentaries on art, objects and society. Some inklings arrived with the Italian anti-design movement, and in particular the outlandish furnishings in polyurethane produced by Turin-based manufacturer Gufram in the late 1960s and early

Lockheed Lounge

The London-based Australian Marc Newson is the only industrial designer represented by one of the most exclusive of modern art galleries, Gagosian. He has designed for upmarket brands such as Hermès and Louis Vuitton, and his work is scattered across major museums. At Apple, he was brought on board by Jony Ive to work on the company's much anticipated watch. But his most expensive work is of earlier vintage. In 1986, he created the Lockheed Lounge chaise longue, a startlingly unusual design made from fibreglass and thin, riveted aluminium plates, constructed 'the exact same way you'd create a surfboard'. Commissioned by Sydney art gallery Roslyn Oxley9, only a handful were made, and they immediately became highly collectable. Philippe Starck gave his seal of approval by putting one in the lobby of the Paramount Hotel, New York, during his glamorous refurbishment of its interiors in 1990. Three years later, one even featured in a music video for Madonna. And, in 2015, an example was sold at auction in London for just shy of £2.5 million, the highest price for a design object by a living designer. The Lockheed Lounge may or may not be art, but it certainly achieves comparable price tags.

1970s. Challenging what furniture could be, these ranged from a human-sized Cactus coatstand to the iconic Pratone seat, with support for the human body provided by 42 tall, flexible blades of grass. One figure emerging out of anti-design proved particularly influential, Ettore Sottsass, who went on to found the Memphis Group. He and his associates designed furniture reflecting eclectic cultures, spiritualism, symbols and even kitsch to create wildly influential, but somewhat confusing, lamps, sideboards and clocks, with a tendency towards bold geometries, decorated laminates and intriguing colours, which gained a wide celebrity following.

Gradually, figures such as the British Israeli industrial designer Ron Arad emerged out of design itself, further fraying the boundaries with art. His works ranged across practical chairs, to highly impractical, if intriguing ones, formed from car seats or inflatable cushions, and on to large public sculptures.

Expanding the dialogue

But design art's full flowering is of more recent origin. In part, it relates to the emergence of such highly intellectual takes as critical design and adversarial design, which seek to create prototypes questioning, among other things, not only the nature of design's role in society, but also the nature of society itself. Mark Shepard's *CCD-Me-Not Umbrella* (2009) is an example of adversarial design, protecting the user against surveillance with flickering LED lights. Market-leading art fair Art Basel embraced design, in all its many faces, in the early 2000s, followed by the establishment of major galleries such as Paris's Galerie Kreo and New York's Friedman Benda. The latter treats design as fine art, ripping off the plaster of usefulness and exhibiting designers in order 'to expand the dialogue in design and explore perspectives that have previously been marginalized'. It can occasionally be hard to ascertain quite which questions are being asked, dialogues expanded and perspectives explored by such sculptural and distinctly uncomfortable designs – it's best not to name names – but the same accusations could probably be made of art itself.

The condensed idea
Design that asks questions

41 Open-source Design

Virtually all design has, at some point, been proprietary, authored, copyrighted, patented – from Thomas Edison's incandescent light bulb to Douglas Engelbart's computer mouse – mainly with a view to financial gain. Some would argue that this is necessary, encouraging investment in innovation, expanding knowledge, fuelling creativity and driving economic growth. Others feel that it doesn't need to be this way, especially given design's claim to be a force for good in the world.

Open-source design represents an alternative approach whereby specialist knowledge, and its outcomes, are shared for free, creating a culture of cooperation that benefits all – those sharing the information, those accessing and adapting it, and the end user – adding circularity and democracy to the design process. Although largely associated with the digital world, it is a principle that extends into the physical realm, often intersecting the two. Moreover, because open source implies consent from the originator or rights holder, it stands on firmer ground than its cousin, hacking (see page 184).

Opening up

The open-source movement is about sharing specialist knowledge, but that is by no means a new concept – the dissemination of sewing patterns in the 19th century allowed people to create clothes that were otherwise beyond their financial reach. If that was an innovation principally accessed by women, another iteration, the do-it-yourself explosion from the mid-20th century, started as a male-dominated one. Through a simple set of instructions (and the emergence of handy new materials such as chipboard and medium-density fibreboard, or MDF), it became simpler for amateur enthusiasts to build furniture, sheds and kitchens – even fundamentally change the layout of their homes – through their own efforts.

But it was the rapid development of software in the 1980s that turned open-source into a movement. Starting with GNU – the name being an acronym for 'GNU's not Unix' – initiated in 1983 by American programmer Richard Stallman to create a free operating system, it expanded significantly with the Linux project launched by Finnish student Linus Torvalds in 1991, and later with Mozilla and

Apache. Virtually all major technology companies, from Apple and IBM to Amazon and Google, have used open-source software in one form or another, and all of these, and more, have released source code for certain of their projects. In parallel, the launch of the World Wide Web in the early 1990s is perhaps the greatest of all open-source projects, thanks to its pioneer Tim Berners-Lee's determination to gift his creation to the world.

During the development of GNU, Richard Stallman evolved the concept of 'copyleft'. Under this legal framework, copyright owners grant others the freedom to use their work – adapting it, copying it, sharing it – but under strict conditions. In particular, any resulting work must also be available under a copyleft licence. In 1998, the Open Source Initiative was founded to advocate for the movement and, via the Open Source Definition, develop agreed standards around which software licences could be considered compatible with open-source principles – their widespread adoption has helped put the resulting software on a secure legal footing.

> Copying all or parts of a program is as natural to a programmer as breathing, and as productive. It ought to be as free.
>
> Richard Stallman, *The GNU Manifesto*, 1985

There have, of course, been problems along the way, given the thorny nature of intellectual property, with disgruntled copyright holders striking back or open-source developers seeing their work being put to commercial ends. Projects can suffer from funding problems, usability issues and community exhaustion, particularly when it comes to maintenance. The impact of AI software development is also adding uncertainties to the mix, benefiting efficiency and maintenance, but throwing up quality and copyright issues, such as open-source code being absorbed into proprietary programs. A debate has also raged between those who see a conflict between the open-source concept, with its priorities and restrictions, and total freedom. Stallman, for example, has noted that 'Open source is a development methodology; free software is a social movement.'

Open source goes physical

Gradually, the open-source concept has expanded beyond the virtual, with concepts of 'open design', 'open making' and 'open manufacturing' evolving from the early 2000s, along with the 'design global, manufacture local' movement. On offer is a more sustainable decentralized model of production, allowing individuals to realize projects themselves, no longer reliant on third-party suppliers and manufacturers with their associated costs, financial and environmental. Platforms such as GrabCAD and Thingiverse host communities creating and sharing millions of free downloadable models – facilitating both collaboration and customization – which can often be fabricated using computer-controlled machining tools and 3D printers.

Adopting a more commercial approach, British-based company Opendesk allows users to choose from a wide range of furniture designs, some customizable, that can be made around the world by

Autoprogettazione?

Enzo Mari was an Italian Modernist artist and designer, who also happened to be a Marxist. Believing that designers have substantial social and ethical responsibilities, and concerned by the industry's increasingly consumerist direction, in 1974 he published *Autoprogettazione?* (which translates as 'self-design?'), sending it out on request for the cost of postage. A DIY manual par excellence, it provides instructions and blueprints allowing makers with no specialized training to build 19 simple pieces of furniture, using little more than standard planks of wood, nails and a hammer. The plain forms of these everyday items were intended to express their function and construction, employing a simple design language that he hoped would encourage people to embark on their own independent journeys of furniture-making, establishing a closer relationship with materials, objects and production in the process. In his democratization of design – constructing an equal, reciprocal relationship between designer and user based on a shared set of values – Mari was a pioneer of pre-digital open-source design.

licensed makers using digital fabrication, cutting out both shipping and middlemen. According to co-founder Joni Steiner: 'When you have the right digital design tools you can question the 20th-century model of manufacturing – the design and the making. Therefore, you can create much more local, human-scale social supply chains.'

Where next?

Inevitably, there are those prepared to use open-source design malevolently. The proliferation of free-access designs for firearms is a prime example, with hundreds of thousands of downloads of the first – for a 3D-printed pistol named the Liberator – within days of its release in 2013. But it is to be hoped that these are outweighed by those seeking to do good, as with recent efforts to create modular open-source shelters for refugee camps, develop open-source prosthetic limbs or even provide downloadable plans for machines that recycle household plastic into everyday items. As yet, progress is slow, but such idealistic start-up projects are beginning to produce concrete results.

Open source is not a panacea. Even in programming, it can be an exclusive club, requiring specific sets of skills and equipment, and significant resources, thus it clusters in universities and tech hubs. Nonetheless, it harbours formidable potential for collaboration, creativity and flexibility, as well as offering a challenge to corporate hegemony. At its best, it puts brilliant design capabilities into new hands. And most of its exponents are dedicated to design for the public good, applying their knowledge in pursuit of Modernism's long-standing goal of improving lives across society.

The condensed idea
Setting design free

42 Circular Design

Green design has been around for a while, doing good and attracting cynicism along the way. Increasingly, however, focus has shifted towards circular design, which provides a more complete approach to reshaping our design and manufacturing sectors, and our relationship with the environment.

The circular economy was first posited in the 1960s, gained traction in the 1990s, and today is increasingly seen by national governments, international organizations and major research institutions as a necessary basis for survival on the planet. Its rise has been accelerated by the Ellen MacArthur Foundation, established by the British sailor in 2010, which describes the circular economy as 'a system where materials never become waste and nature is regenerated. In a circular economy, products and materials are kept in circulation through processes like maintenance, reuse, refurbishment, remanufacture, recycling and composting.' It's an important vision, but one facing forbidding political, economic and cultural challenges that some fear will never be overcome.

A new relationship with the planet

Over the last century, design has played a key role in building a linear 'take-make-dispose' economy, contributing to production and consumption models in which natural resources are extracted, transported and processed to make goods that are soon discarded, generating waste along the way. Fears around this cavalier attitude to the planet, and our presumption of primacy in the natural world, were already being voiced in the 1940s. American naturalist Aldo Leopold wrote in 1949: 'We abuse land because we regard it as a commodity belonging to us. When we see land as a community to which we belong, we may begin to use it with love and respect.' In this, Leopold was echoing the beliefs of indigenous communities in North America and beyond, for instance

> The object of the next industrial revolution is to ensure that there will be no such thing as waste, on the basis that waste is simply some substance that we do not yet have the wit to use.
>
> Athelstan Spilhaus, 1970

the very personal relationship of the Maori people with the environment as a sustainer of life, in which all things are interdependent, and which everyone has a duty to preserve for future generations.

In the 1960s, the first images of Earth were captured from space, highlighting its fragility and the interconnected nature of all life, and leading to the concept of 'Spaceship Earth'. Its fullest and most eloquent expression came from American economist Kenneth Boulding, who posited the existence of 'cowboy' and 'spaceship' economies, with the former 'symbolic of the illimitable plains and also associated with reckless, exploitative, romantic, and violent behaviour', and the latter a closed system in which 'the earth has become a single spaceship, without unlimited reservoirs of anything, either for extraction or for pollution, and in which, therefore, man must find his place in a cyclical ecological system'. In tandem, countercultural movements began to explore a more sustainable future, resulting in such alternative visions as *The Whole Earth Catalog*, first published by Steward Brand in 1968. With a picture of Earth on its cover, the magazine was packed with reviews of books and products that promoted self-sufficiency, kicking off with four volumes by the mercurial American architect Buckminster Fuller.

Circular design today

It took half a century for the concept of Earth as a closed system to shift from a poignant evocation of fragility to an urgent mainstream issue, with major contributions from academics such as Victor Papanek and Athelstan Spilhaus along the way. Today design strategies are finally being formulated for achieving a circular economy, but allocating responsibility, and dividing costs, is a challenge. As a starting point, life-cycle assessments of the consumption of energy and resources in product manufacture, use and disposal are being created, and a growing range of tactics adopted to reduce these 'cradle-to-grave' impacts. Joining the long-standing focus on recycling, which has proven limited in isolation, emphasis is now placed on the durability, reuse, flexibility, sharing, refurbishing, upgrading, repairability and upcycling of products. Supply chains are becoming more transparent, with a pivot towards local materials, while ease of disassembly for recycling and repair is being built into the design of products. Companies are being required to take back

Although economists Kenneth Boulding and Barbara Ward reached the printed page earlier with the concept of Spaceship Earth, a bigger splash was made by American architect Buckminster Fuller, pioneer of the geodesic dome. His 1969 *Operating Manual for Spaceship Earth* famously stated, 'We are all astronauts', and portrayed the planet as a tiny, speeding sphere in the vastness of space, 'so extraordinarily well invented and designed that to our knowledge humans have been on board it for two million years not even knowing that they were on board a ship'. In Fuller's view, humanity's abuse of this 'extraordinary chemical energy-interchanging system', constantly refuelled by the sun, required a de-politicized world order, with equal distribution of wealth and an embrace of computers as the 'evolutionary antibody' to the extinction of humanity.

The book acted, in part, as a promotional tool for his proposal of a World Resources Center in Carbondale, Illinois, that would comprise an enormous, rentable computer, which was never realized – perhaps fortuitously, as the internet soon superseded its basic premise.

goods at the end of their useful life and are banned from placing some waste materials in landfill. Consumers are also being given the right to have their products repaired, or to purchase goods as a service, shifting the burden of maintenance and repair onto the seller. Technology can play a role in removing physical items from the environment, reducing manufacturing and transport waste.

As yet, such approaches are proving far from complete answers to establishing a circular economy, which comes with significant financial, cultural and political costs. Public policy and global co-operation will be required to overcome these, before the long-term economic and environmental benefits can be unlocked. One suggestion is that companies will need to reconceive their business models, making profits not through the sale of individual products, but through cultivating an efficient flow of resources and materials through their business over time. A behavioural shift on the part of consumers will be required, and even more on the part of designers, with their influence on the materials and processes of product manufacture. To play their part in achieving this shift to a circular economy, they will need to work closely with engineers, politicians, naturalists, economists, anthropologists, financiers, even historians, bringing together professions and industries that have to converse and collaborate to ensure the future of the planet.

The condensed idea
Design that never dies

43 The Touchscreen

There is surely no clearer manifestation of the intertwining of design and contemporary life than the mobile phone – as evidenced by that moment of sheer terror when one is temporarily misplaced. It was way back in 1973 that the first mobile phone call was made, in New York by a Motorola engineer to a friend and counterpart at AT&T. The technology took years to bed in, however, and by the end of the 1980s, the chunky units of that period were still largely the preserve of business. But a decade later, the age of the smartphone was upon us, with the development (though not public release) of the Ericsson GS88 'Penelope' in 1997. Here was a phone that offered not only call facilities, but additional functions mirroring those of computers, including access to email and other 'personal assistant' services. In 1999, an *Economist* editorial would claim: 'Mobile phones are rapidly becoming ubiquitous; now they are about to become multipurpose, too, offering everything from internet access to an organized life.'

Over the next few years, that prediction was realized, the mobile no longer merely a mode of communication, but a personal organizer, receptacle of memories, entertainment centre, font of all knowledge and status symbol – not to mention a massive distraction. And the reason? The touchscreen, undoubtedly one of the most significant design innovations of the modern era. Before 2007, mobiles were condensed, awkward little devices comprising a keypad and a tiny screen suitable for calls and little more – unless you were a Blackberry owner, blessed with the ability to type on a keyboard crammed across 10cm (4in). To have access to the entirety of the virtual world, sitting there in your pocket, with no need for a separate screen, keyboard, mouse or cable, was almost inconceivable. Today, it is barely worth a mention.

Getting started

A touchscreen is one that incorporates both input (a user's touch) via a touch panel, and output, serving as a visual display. Today, they are common not just in smartphones, but in all manner of electronic devices, from laptops to museum displays, cashpoints to medical equipment. They permit a level of rapid and intuitive interaction that had long been the preserve of science fiction, even in the 'digital stone age' of the keyboard and mouse.

The touchscreen's genesis is a long one. In 1946, a patent was granted in the United States for a 'Direct Light Pen' that could be used with a cathode-ray tube so that simple symbols might be 'drawn' onto a live televised broadcast. Then, in 1962, A&T developed a more sophisticated variation, again using a stylus for input. But it was three years later, in Britain, that Eric Johnson of the Royal Radar Establishment reported his work on a capacitive touchscreen that was the first to be finger-driven – technology later put to use in an air-traffic-control context.

At this stage, the battle was on between resistive screens that were responsive to applied pressure, and capacitive screens that made use of electrical properties within the human body to provide input – the latter ultimately winning out in most modern consumer technology, even if the former still boasts certain practical applications in industry and medicine, particularly when gloves are involved. The early 1980s were another rich period of development, with leaps forward in the technology of multitouch screens that can recognize multiple points of contact at the same time. This opened up new commercial vistas, but ones that would take years to come to fruition.

The advent of the iPhone

In 1994, IBM released its Simon Personal Communicator, widely regarded as the first touchscreen smartphone, but weighty, expensive, and so far ahead of its time that both the technology and the market needed to catch up. The release of Apple's first iPhone in 2007, with its multitouch screen, confirmed that the concept had truly come of age. Apple boss Steve Jobs announced its imminent arrival amid enormous excitement in January that year. In fact, word

Every once in a while a revolutionary product comes along that changes everything.
Steve Jobs, 2007

had emerged just a few weeks earlier of another touchscreen phone, a collaboration between LG and Prada, but the iPhone effectively stole its thunder. Launched that June, this 'revolutionary and magical product', in Job's words, arrived with a 9-cm (3½-in) multitouch display that rendered hardware buttons virtually redundant. Even with its hefty starting price of $499, the technology did not disappoint, allowing users to tap, slide, drag, pinch and rotate as they explored the device's extravagant array of capabilities.

With each new iteration, the iPhone has introduced new technical developments, accompanied by perfectly orchestrated hype. For instance, since 2015, it has incorporated modern haptic feedback technology that helps simulate the sensation of features like physical buttons to provide a more tactile experience. Far from the only touchscreen smartphone on a flooded market, and joined in 2010 by its tablet sibling, the iPad, it is fair to say that the iPhone remains the gamechanger, with global sales heading towards three billion units.

The future

Touchscreens are still grabbing headlines today, sometimes for becoming more flexible and foldable, or even transparent; sometimes for becoming ever larger, perhaps wall-sized, accommodating multiple users, and turning creativity into a collaborative activity. Their future certainly looks exciting, but it's worth remembering just how young the technology is. The long-term impact of having one of these portals stuffed in a back pocket is unclear. Common sense, as well as ongoing research, certainly suggests that there are risks around excessive screentime, particularly for children – and social media isn't helping. There are also risks with the ever more sophisticated incorporation of touch into interfaces, reported as increasing educational engagement, but also 'purchase intention'. There is much to celebrate in the ingenuity of touchscreens, and the intertwining of design and life they have facilitated, but their place in our future needs careful consideration. Or, more realistically, we just need to take advice from that mountain of unread self-help books, and periodically step away from the phone.

The condensed idea
Touching the future

44 Feminist Design

Although it has a long history, gaining prominence in universities in the 1970s, the profile of Feminist design was given a significant boost by Caroline Criado Perez's *Invisible Women: Exposing Data Bias in a World Designed for Men* in 2019. Alongside wider perspectives on injustices faced by women in society, the book exposed how product design embodies and perpetuates discrimination, relying on pre-existing data gathered and utilized in problematic ways. From voice-recognition software to crash-test dummies, 'the one-size-fits-men approach to supposedly gender-neutral products is disadvantaging women', and can be highly dangerous – for instance, when safety features are tailored to the male anatomy alone. Today, design penetrates the entirety of our lives, and these biases are now being implanted into code. As artificial intelligence plays a bigger and bigger role in our decision-making and our lives, this embedded discrimination may prove very hard to dislodge.

Valuing people and practices

For decades, women have been ignored as both creators and consumers of design, and one of the most visible aspects of Feminist design today is the foregrounding of lost or under-recognized designers, from Arts and Crafts figures such as Agnes Northrop and May Morris, to Modernist pioneers such as Eileen Gray, Charlotte Perriand and Clara Porset. Giving belated recognition for their talent is certainly important, decisively discrediting archaic prejudices about women's clarity and creativity. Feminist design history also foregrounds such pioneering thinkers as the American Charlotte Perkins Gilman who, from the 1890s, sought to overturn existing social orders dictating women's domestic roles, proposing alternative structures in their place.

To really overturn past discrimination, however, this recognition needs to extend beyond design's traditional obsession with lone figures, to women working in spheres considered less prestigious, or who designed collaboratively. Whether in homes, on factory floors or in drawing studios, 'women's work' often entailed long hours, reduced access to education and advancement, limited pay and minimal recognition. Within design, many of the outcomes – embroidery, ceramics, fashion and illustration – have widely been perceived as decorative, in contrast to the prestige associated with creating objects for mass production. In many ways, this was intensified by Modernism, with its single-minded focus on industrial design, its belief in linear 'progress', and a focus on universal application. With a consequent disdain for 'crafts', the vital roles the latter played in practical, economic and social terms were largely ignored – as were the clues they provide to achieving a better balance with the planet.

Inclusive solutions

These mindsets and prejudices can still be found across design. To address them, studios urgently need to ensure the diversity of their recruitment and the inclusivity of their practices and environments. They also need to design for a wider range of users rather than defaulting to norms. The lack of women in leadership roles makes both goals harder to achieve – and mentorship harder to provide – but they are essential in order to tackle design's pervading culture successfully. This isn't just a matter of breaking glass ceilings and closing pay gaps in design offices, but also of changing design's self-presentation, with its pervasive focus on individuals and luxury, and its education, which prioritizes simple solutions to complex issues. The result would be a greater diversity – and an undoubted improvement – in the services and products created by designers, benefitting society as a whole.

The entrenched obsession with gendered products is similarly problematic. Many of them make presumptions about women's roles as consumers, with agency over choices of household items or small cars, or a preference for 'female' aesthetics. Pink razors and patterned ballpoint pens often come with excessive packaging, lower production values and higher price points – a practice known as 'shrink it and pink it' – while virtual assistants tend to have female names and personas. Such prejudices are enmeshed in marketing, but also in views about women's role in society. Unpicking them, and the power imbalances they represent and reinforce, is a massive task, and a necessarily

> Feminist design is not just a thing you do; it's how you do every thing.
> Alison Pearce, 2023

political one. Many would suggest that these problems can only be tackled by rebuilding design itself. Drawing on evolving Feminist frameworks, a more collective approach to design could be adopted, allowing diverse views and alternative solutions to co-exist, and taking into consideration a wider group of practitioners and users, with a focus on community and care. Priorities would be shifted towards such issues as climate, food security and sustainability, which impact on women and marginalized groups disproportionately, and also towards social values and responsibilities rather than form and function.

Positive results

This focus on questioning norms and embracing open endings can sometimes feel insubstantial in the result-driven, one-size-fits-all world of design. Certainly, many Feminist designs are 'speculative', asking questions, suggesting alternative futures, and provoking wider conversations, rather than seeking single solutions. But equally important are incremental changes with longer timeframes, many of which will have application for all marginalized communities,

Charlotte Perriand

In 1927, on visiting the studio of leading Modernist architect Charles-Édouard Jeanneret, known as Le Corbusier, the young French designer Charlotte Perriand was turned away with the dismissive 'We don't embroider cushions here'. Having conclusively proved her talent at that winter's Salon d'Automne exhibition, she was invited back to help the studio create 'interior equipment' that would match the revolutionary furniture emerging from the Bauhaus. The results included the famed movable curved chaise longue in chromed steel and pony skin, an iconic exercise in glamour later designated the LC4, Perriand's name having slipped away. She carved out a successful career as an architect and designer, but it is only in the last decade that full recognition of her track record, in the 1920s and beyond, has finally been achieved.

ensuring Feminist design is not an inward-looking practice. For example, efforts are currently being pursued to make coding more accessible, increasing proficiency beyond its present male-dominated enclaves, turning it into a more collaborative, inclusive process, and warding off the engrained biases of which Caroline Criado Perez has warned. Employing Feminist insights, there is greater potential for technology and design to achieve positive and pluralist ends that help to confront the environmental and social challenges of the contemporary world, and also imagine and deliver a better one – a goal that design has long set itself.

The condensed idea
Redesigning design

45 **Social Design**

Social design is the umbrella term for design whose principal goal is to improve the social good, above – although not necessarily exclusive of – any other concerns, including commercial ones. It can range across service design, user-experience design and product design but, given the obligation to bring about positive social change, those involved carry moral and ethical burdens that many other design practitioners do not have to consider. Correspondingly, a successful project can achieve positive outcomes that are a welcome change from design's typical social and environmental impacts.

Geared to addressing complex challenges, it is a mode of design most regularly practised in governmental, charitable and social sectors, or by social entrepreneurs, although it is becoming increasingly appealing to commercial businesses aware of the value of acquiring a reputation for social engagement. Closely related to such areas as human-centred design and design thinking, but set apart by its dedication to a social agenda, the practice remains very much in its infancy, with few hard-and-fast rules, and an impressively broad field of ambition. Various theoretical approaches have emerged over the years. Some pursue a fusion of social and commercial demands as a means to successful outcomes, such as Stanford University's model of design-thinking. Others, for example, the new materialist model initiated by Jan Boelen and Michael Kaethler, argue that social design is inextricably linked to the material realm, giving practitioners a strong ethical responsibility to challenge the wider status quo, and consider the lasting repercussions of their work in both material and social realms. However, the participatory aspect – engaging with stakeholders to create solutions that emerge out of communities, and are often enacted by them – is almost universally seen as key to the success of social design.

Victor Papanek

The first hints of social design emerged in the 1960s, segueing neatly with the era's counter-cultural movement. Its undisputed godfather was Austrian-born Victor Papanek, who escaped to the United States after his homeland's annexation by Hitler in 1938. Papanek, an industrial designer, teacher and prolific theorist, led a critique of consumerism and demanded a new mode of design that put wider society at its heart. He argued that designers ought to be aware of the overall consequences of their work, not least in terms of ecological impact, and championed the notion of designing for need rather than want, addressing issues of inclusion, social justice and sustainability.

Despite some persuasive proposals – the Tin Can Radio, constructed from a juice can, with paraffin wax and a wick as a power source, was intended to bring radio to isolated rural communities at a cost of under 10 cents – few of Papanek's designs reached production. However, his 1971 book, *Design for the Real World: Human Ecology and Social Change*, was a game-changer, initially dividing the design community, but fundamentally changing the discourse around the discipline, so that it became accepted as one with political agency. From the designer's choice of materials to the identification of their target market and the methods used to meet that market's needs, every step in the design journey was now understood to have repercussions across society.

> The only important thing about design is how it relates to people.
> Victor Papanek

Papanek's influence has been prevalent in design culture ever since, and is explicit in the work of many recent artists and designers such as Catherine Sarah Young, Gabriel Ann Maher and Tomás Saraceno. It can also be seen in specific projects using design to find effective, affordable, community-driven solutions to enduring problems, including Peter Muckle's emergency saddle for transporting pregnant women in remote parts of the world, Matt McClumpha's Pure Water device that uses natural sunlight to purify water, Pettie Petzer and Johan Jonke's Hippo Roller that has improved water transportation in rural Africa, and Illac Diaz's harnessing of the Moser lamp (see box).

Moving forwards

As social design has become more embedded as a discipline, both its practice and theory have become more sophisticated. In particular, the husband-and-wife team of Victor and Sylvia Margolin has considered its implications for social services, health and education provision, developing new methods incorporating data analysis and user feedback. In acknowledging the designer's ability to 'address human problems on a broad scale and contribute to social well-being', they have pushed for a professionalization of the field, distancing it from ideas of charity and voluntary work, while also acknowledging its divergence from traditional corporate models.

The Moser lamp

Significant numbers of people in the world live without reliable electricity, making it difficult to guarantee even basics like house lighting. During Brazil's energy crisis in 2001–02, mechanic Alfredo Moser grew tired of blackouts and decided to address the problem. He invented the solar bottle bulb, which uses a standard plastic bottle filled with water and bleach to refract solar light and provide interior lighting equivalent to a 40–60 watt incandescent bulb. His open-source design was picked up by Illac Diaz, who launched a project in the Philippines in 2011 called Liter of Light. Within four years, a million bulbs were installed across the country, each of them with the potential to last for five years. A brilliant practical solution for communities that had literally been living in the dark, it inspired similar initiatives throughout the world.

Proposing a new 'social model' for design in 2002, the Margolins wrote: 'The primary purpose of design for the market is creating products for sale. Conversely, the foremost intent of social design is the satisfaction of human needs. However, we don't propose the "market model" and the "social model" as binary opposites, but instead view them as two poles of a continuum. The difference is defined by the priorities of the commission rather than by a method of production or distribution.' More recently, their position has evolved to suggest that, in a crisis-ridden world, the design community needs to embrace more responsibility, and 'recognize its own power as a collective agent of change and undertake a radical re-thinking of how we can live'.

This change in scope reflects criticism that social design applies the tools of the existing system to tinker around the edges. Rather than addressing specific problems, it is argued, design should be confronting society's fundamental issues, and questioning its own role in perpetuating them. Yet, given its current burst of productivity, and the transformative projects that have resulted, social design looks set to remain among the most important areas of the discipline for the forseeable future.

The condensed idea
Design for the greater good

46 Hacking

When it comes to hacking, there are two primary schools of thought. For many – perhaps most – it is synonymous with the sort of malevolent computer system hack that sees social media accounts taken over, or credit card details appropriated. But for others, it stands as an innovative culture that adapts products, services or systems for positive ends, better answering a wide range of human needs. As such, hacking can be seen as merely the latest iteration of age-old traditions of modification that have long facilitated human progress – and one that is key to its continuation.

Rise of the hacker

The term 'hacking' seemingly first appeared in the 1955 minutes of the Tech Model Railroad Club at the Massachusetts Institute of Technology (MIT), referring to inventive solutions to problems with its substantial track. Increasingly, hacking involved adaptations of the circuits making the trains run, and the club began to develop sophisticated programs to that end, making use of the university's powerful computers. The term gradually spread among academics and enthusiasts at MIT and beyond seeking to expand the intended operations of computer systems in unexpected ways. In those early days, hacking was an inventive, explorative activity, dominated by collaborative communities and egalitarian mindsets, with participants sharing knowledge and skills to mutual benefit.

Probably the first celebrity hacker was John Draper (aka Captain Crunch), arrested in 1972 for involvement in 'phone phreaking', including his infiltration of a large telephone network using a whistle given away in Cap'n Crunch cereal boxes – a model of hacker ingenuity. It would not be until the end of the 1980s, however, that cyber hacking arrived in earnest, when academic Robert Morris unleashed one of the first known computer worms in order, he claimed, to measure the size of the internet. In practice, it worked to highlight its extreme vulnerability.

By the 1990s, hacking's darker sides – financial greed, criminal ambition, a desire to obtain confidential information or spread misinformation, or simply disrupt for its own sake – were becoming ever more apparent. But it was also starting to enter grey areas, acting as a tool of political and social activism (epitomized by the Anonymous group), civil disobedience and, as famously exemplified by WikiLeaks, whistle-blowing. Whether malevolent, benevolent or somewhere in between, hacking was now firmly established as part of the technological landscape.

Inventing hackathons

From its earliest days, the fraternal nature of hacking – for long stretches of its history, it has been a largely male pursuit – involved the real-time sharing of hacks. In the 1990s, this evolved into time-limited hackathons, many of them with a libertarian agenda. Despite those anti-establishment vibes, the concentrated creativity of such events proved too enticing for businesses and institutions to ignore. From computer-games developers right through to NASA, a well-managed hackathon has become a go-to method for discovering flaws that have evaded in-house teams, or arriving at innovative solutions and ideas that move projects, and knowledge, forward. By offering incentives, a new layer of problem-solving is generated, ensuring that relevant talent is working on the inside rather than the outside.

Mother and baby

A great example of benevolent hacker culture is the Make the Breast Pump Not Suck project, which emerged from a 2014 hackathon involving 150 designers, developers, parents and babies who collaborated in search of better breast pumps, nursing environments and support systems for breastfeeding mothers. In an area of care that is frequently not as nurturing as it ought to be – and replete with devices poorly designed for women, often by men – the collective takes existing technology and seeks ways to improve it in a concerted programme of what it describes as 'equity-based design'.

The male-dominated, competitive nature of hacking brings with it a raft of problems, and makes it an intimidating arena for women, minorities and newcomers. This lack of inclusivity can be reflected and perpetuated in the solutions offered, making the recent expansion of Feminist hackerspaces – physical and virtual – an important development, helping more women feel comfortable in the hacking ecosystem, allowing their creativity to flourish.

Cyberspace to reality

To an extent, hacking has slipped its cyber heritage, with hackathons and hackerspaces bringing together experts and amateurs across disciplines to tackle problems in real-world design. There is a clear overlap with the maker movement, in which communities of creators, entrepreneurs and inventors come together in well-equipped collaborative workspaces to share information, materials, tools and skills to prototype products, work on joint projects, disassemble technology and rebuild it in new forms, or just create it from scratch.

Hacking's principles of playfulness, innovation and freedom, as well as its commitment to solving specific challenges, are evident in the growing online community of IKEA hackers utilizing standard furniture from the Swedish giant, adapting it to meet their bespoke requirements, and expressing their individuality along the way. On specialist websites, downloads are available offering free hacks to any number of problems, recognized or otherwise, whether files for machining key components for workshop tools, or for 3D-printing connectors joining together Lego blocks to Lincoln Logs.

Hacking can be a force for good in parts of the world where access to high-cost finished products is limited, extending the potential of available components and technologies instead. Cameroonian designer Arthur Zang, for instance, has created a low-cost mobile heart monitor, the Cardiopad, co-opting bluetooth and mobile phone networks to allow isolated,

> Ultimately, hacking gives people a voice. Hacking creates new realities, options and possibilities from those we are given. . .It offers forth the notion of a democratization of design, by enabling the end user to be part of the process and not only on the receiving end of it.
>
> Scott Burnham, *Design Hacking*, 2010

rural practitioners to instantly send data to hospitals for analysis. Such hacks are vital tools to overcoming infrastructural shortfalls and materially improving lives.

Changing design

Support for the hacking movement is now coming from authoritative design voices, including Konstantin Grcic, perhaps the most celebrated industrial designer at work today. In a 2022 interview, he said, 'Hacking is a form of appropriation and customization. . .It's a creative act. I find the open dimension of it interesting – you are challenged to engage with a product, to extend it, to grow it, to hack it. A commercial product that is in some way unfinished and only becomes finished through the intervention of the user – that's a paradigm shift.'

The abuse of hacking for criminal or acquisitive purposes shouldn't negate its potential as a liberating creative tool – one that replaces uniformity and control with choice and freedom. Promoting problem-solving as an aspiration in its own right, hacking strips away decades of rules. Not least, it provides a corrective to the myth of the omniscient designer – the consumer is no longer a passive recipient but a self-reliant participant with agency in the design process. Eventually, it may even be that companies and customers routinely accept hacking as a valid form of interaction, leading to a closer and more sustainable relationship between owners, manufacturers and products, while expanding the life and capabilities of those products.

The condensed idea
Taking control of design

47 Design Activism

In modern terms, design activism is a relatively recent concept, focused on creating practical, inventive and accessible means of generating change, and reclaiming power from the powerful, often through disruptive actions. From a longer perspective, design has been fomenting change for centuries. An early example might be the posting of the 95 Theses by Martin Luther on a church door in Wittenberg in 1517. This attack on the practices and theology of the Catholic Church was printed in moveable type on a mechanical printing press, invented by Johannes Gutenberg in the previous century, allowing for its distribution right across Europe. In the 19th and early 20th centuries, further advances in printing technology – steam-powered presses and offset printing – allied with the mechanization of paper-making helped to make such politically charged calls for change universal. Many of the results have become iconic political images, whether the imposing posters pushing China's Great Leap Forward or the Black Power movement in the 1960s, or Shepard Fairey's canonical *Hope* poster, created as an act of grassroots support for Barack Obama's 2008 presidential campaign, which drew on those same Chinese Communist posters of the 1960s.

Beyond paper

Design activism has been a key tool in campaigns for equality. The abolitionist 'Am I Not a Man and a Brother' emblem, which first appeared on porcelain medallions manufactured by mass-production pioneer Josiah Wedgwood in the 1780s, spread around the world on plates, metal tokens and even hair pins. Suffragette flags and pins (originally featuring bluebirds) didn't stick as symbols – in Britain at least, purple banners proved the lasting image from the protest marches of the 1900s. Conversely, the rainbow flag created by San Francisco artist Gilbert Baker in 1978, originally designed to celebrate members of the gay and lesbian political movement, remains a potent rallying call in ever-evolving forms across marginalized groups. In a reaction against the ubiquity of the Stars and Stripes during the United States' bicentennial celebrations two years earlier, Baker designed an icon that fundamentally reshaped contemporary notions of what a flag could be – not an aggressive testament to patriotism, but an exultant symbol of collectivity and progress. In so doing, he revealed just how powerful design can be in reshaping our social and political environments, and also in reimagining the roles that familiar objects can play in our lives.

Taking it to the streets

Creating symbols has been a major role for designers in political movements, but today design activism increasingly means direct intervention in the physical environment. In the 1990s, streets were reclaimed – temporarily blocking cars to make space on roads for community parties with sandpits and food stalls – and in the 2010s, financial and political centres were occupied to highlight inequality and democratic decay. Both movements indicated the impact of such disruptive actions in highlighting and counteracting the escalating link between power and public space.

Design plays a role in such activities, but sometimes in unexpected ways that endure when the encampment has gone, or involve subtler reappropriations of public space. In 1997, Spanish architect Santiago Cirugeda's request to build a playground for local children in Seville was denied by government officials, so he obtained temporary permission to place a skip in front of his house, then installed a see-saw inside. He has employed the tactic since to create what he calls 'urban reserves' that involve acts of resistance to authority. In his Scaffolding project, for instance, a request to erect scaffolds to remove graffiti is used as a pretext to add extra rooms to houses in cramped urban areas.

This transformation of a city space into a public amenity through a design hack – working within the system's rules, both explicit and unspoken, but refashioning them to alternative purposes – has been taken up by many designers. The worldwide Park(ing) movement, originating in San Francisco, expands the public realm in cities by appropriating parking spaces to create recreational oases of green, but has become a little more combative in recent years. Such schemes can become community projects, as in the installation of libraries in phone booths, but can also also extend to community workshops and studios.

Confronting power

One recent object that stands at the intersection of protest tool and installation art is the inflatable cobblestone designed by Artúr van Balen of Tools for Action. Reminiscent of inflatables employed in Italian protests against the Vietnam War in the 1960s, these large silver cubes evolved from the group's own 12m-long (39ft) silver hammer utilized at a climate protest in Cancún, Mexico, in 2010, which received widespread press coverage. The inflatables act as playful, interactive objects at occupations and marches, referencing the appropriation of cobblestones from streets in protests across the ages. But they also provide protection and barriers against violence at moments of confrontation, fulfilling the role of 'practical frivolity'.

Simple tripods of bamboo can provide an effective, affordable and rapid means of physically occupying and disrupting activity at major locations. They also make the protestor sitting at the intersection above – often wielding a message-bearing flag to counter media misinterpretation – both conspicuous and difficult to remove, particularly when the base of the tripod is protected by metal fencing. More sophisticated means of inhabiting space include tall beacons created from complex networks of bamboo and metal cable, quickly erected and supported by their tensional integrity – tensegrity – to increase both height and prominence. Sometimes tarpaulins and boxes are even installed beneath to allow for sleeping and storage, and protestors 'lock on' to each other, slowing down removal. Many of these ever-evolving techniques are shared with other protest movements around the world via 'how-to' guides and apps.

Much design activism is ephemeral – a temporary intervention intended to make an immediate visual and physical impression, helping to shift the needle on major issues, living on only in political and social impact, and lodging in both media and memory. But it is a means for designers to untangle themselves, even if temporarily, from the discipline's enmeshing in contemporary power structures, using their unique skills to make contributions to their communities and causes. And it is likely to become ever more widespread as a design practice as the challenges facing society become increasingly urgent.

The condensed idea
Design as a political act

48 Critical Design

Designers, and design movements, have long taken critical positions. Through the handcrafted simplicity and practicality of their furnishings, the protagonists of the Arts and Crafts movement censured the degeneracy of Victorian design and manufacture, in terms of quality, ethics and aesthetics. Modernism, and then Postmodernism, claimed a positive, progressive engagement with modern life, loudly repudiating alternative approaches. And radical practices of the 1960s such as Archigram and Superstudio invented fantastical, utopian projects to challenge established institutions. Critical design, however, raises fundamental questions about the role of products in everyday life, the values and achievements of design, and their relationship with society as a whole.

Beyond affirmative design

The term 'critical design' was coined in 1999 by Anthony Dunne, who had founded the collaborative practice Dunne & Raby with Fiona

Raby five years earlier, after the pair spent an inspiring period working in Tokyo. Both are graduates of (and were, for a long time, professors at) London's powerhouse design school, the Royal College of Art, equipping them with a full gamut of traditional design skills. However, they evolved a new approach – one they describe as 'more of an attitude than anything else' – in which design becomes a medium for criticism. The resulting products are not intended to function or to solve problems in the traditional 'affirmative' sense, which acts to reinforce the status quo, but instead 'to question products through products', exploring our assumptions about the role of objects, and of design, in our environment, culture and lives.

The prototypical objects created by Dunne and Raby can be disturbing, for instance a plush, huggable atomic mushroom cloud, designed 'to meet irrational but real needs, in this case, a fear of nuclear annihilation'. This is a bold claim to make of a soft furnishing, making it likely that the real purpose of the cushion is to highlight our misplaced faith that products can solve our personal or systemic problems. Sometimes, their designs are more overtly entertaining, if more scatological. The two adjoining compartments of their Poo Lunch Box are labelled 'Lunch' and 'Poo', turning an everyday object into a blunt question about our future energy needs, and our cultural hang-ups. The immediacy of these products, with their strange familiarity, helps make abstract issues accessible to all, empowering people to engage directly, without mediation by curators and critics.

> Critical design is critical thought translated into materiality. It is about thinking through design rather than through words and using the language and structure of design to engage people.
>
> Anthony Dunne and Fiona Raby, *Speculative Everything*, 2013

Parallel presents and possible futures

It can sometimes be hard to gauge how serious Dunne and Raby are being, yet even their more light-hearted products offer surprisingly acute evocations of a parallel reality: 'We need to move beyond designing for the way things are now and begin to design for how things could be, imagining alternative possibilities and different ways of being and giving tangible form to new values and priorities.' The

Design fiction

Critical design has spawned a range of practices dedicated to exploring the complexities of modern living through design, with names such as 'futures design', 'interrogative design' or, best of all, 'design fiction'. The latter's primary proponent, Julian Bleecker, describes it as creating 'materialized thought experiments'. If design is a creative endeavour in which ideas are explored and realized, then mixing in the imaginative freedom of science fiction can release designers to invent expressive objects that imply sweeping change. Examples include fully realized packaging for insect-based cereals of the future, or an extraordinarily slow messaging device that delivers content in relation to time spent holding and walking with it, capturing the emotions embodied in physical mail. Such playful projects embrace humour and observation but overlap with the real world in a manner that encourages both the suspension of disbelief and the flow of ideas, making fictional futures seem tangible, even probable.

speculative near futures proposed by critical design are often elaborate, and a little dark, yet retain their credibility, thanks to extensive collaboration with other disciplines, from engineering and computer science to sociology and ethnography. This credibility increases the impact of even far-fetched scenarios, making it more likely that we will engage, and change our direction of travel as a result. In the video work *Designs for an Overpopulated Planet: Foragers*, for instance, amateur 'foragers' on the edge of society, confronted by food shortages, create a series of DIY prostheses inspired by other animals' digestive systems to extract nutrition from their degraded urban environment, creating a bottom-up solution to a very possible problem.

Critical design is occasionally classified as conceptual art by critics, as it creates products that appear to lack functionality, disqualifying them from the category of design. Most of its practitioners reject this label, with Dunne stating his preference to show at high-street stores rather than galleries. And perhaps its products do serve functions –

raising questions, communicating ideas and provoking debate. Unfortunately, they are almost always encountered at specialist exhibitions, where the public is small, self-selecting, and with little meaningful influence on general priorities and values. But, within the profession, critical design has certainly expanded understandings of how design and society interact, and started important conversations about the ideologies embedded in design and technology today. The hope is that these understandings and conversations can help us plot a proactive, positive route to a more sustainable future.

The condensed idea
Designed to provoke thought

49 Regenerative Design

It can be hard to know how best to design for sustainability, when no one is sure what a circular economy might look like. The goal is a closed-loop system that mimics the biological ecosystem, with waste material from one process becoming a resource for another. This goal is increasingly seen as fundamental to our future, yet every new product design requires balancing a different set of 'least worst options' that diverge from it, related to anything from local recycling targets to fragile supply chains to global politics.

Providing answers to all these problems may not be realistic, but designers possess skills ideally suited to exploring directions that could help, from an ability to consolidate multiple sources of information and engage with diverse communities and disciplines, to vital experience experimenting with new materials, processes and technologies, and prototyping and trialling the results. At present, complex infrastructures and technologies are being employed in pursuit of sustainability. Regenerative design offers the tantalizing possibility of simply replacing the current industrial ecosystem with a biological one – one in harmony with, and even restorative of, both nature and communities. Designers' creative skillsets will be fundamental to achieving this goal.

Designing with nature

Regenerative design is full of flowery phrases, but for the present it means rethinking our reliance on standard sustainable practices such as recycling, reuse and durability. Instead, materials, processes and products are viewed as agriculture as much as industry, with the transience that implies. Resources are borrowed from the environment rather than removed, avoiding energy-intensive and partial recycling at the end of products' lives. On the contrary, they become an accessible organic resource in their entirety, returned to the soil, replenishing the wider ecosystem and restoring biodiversity in the process. A good example is thatching, for thousands of years a key building technique across the globe. Such traditional crops as straw, reed, palm leaves or seaweed, some of them a byproduct of food production, are harvested to roof houses, helping to sustain natural habitats and local economies. There, they sequester significant amounts of carbon, until replaced after a few decades as they decompose, beginning their transition into a rich fertilizer. Industrialization has reduced thatching to a heritage activity in most countries, but progressive architectural practices are rediscovering it for roofing and cladding, replacing problematic alternatives, including slate, ceramic and asphalt tiles and oil-based insulation products. Similar explorations are taking place with other organic materials – for instance, hemp is being used to manufacture 'hempcrete', a zero-carbon substitute for concrete, and cow manure is being reintroduced into its traditional role as a stabilizer in mud-based building materials.

Root to leaf

When scaling up production of organic materials, industrial techniques are often used for harvesting, drying or processing, while inorganic products are introduced as binding agents, dyes, preservatives or stabilizers. Wood has an important role to play in regenerative design, but also highlights its risks. Intensive forestry degrades environments and involves damaging processes and long-distance transportation, while the resulting timber decomposes slowly, releasing methane as it does so, or is used for non-biodegradable products that include synthetic resins. Efficient use of felled trees is vital, requiring the quantity of material produced to be maximized, and those parts of the tree usually treated as waste to be reconceived as a resource. This 'root to leaf' philosophy is an increasingly

We have to urgently think about how we design to repair and restore our ecosystems. And that can be enabled by bio-based research.
Carole Collet, Central Saint Martins, University of the Arts, London

important strategy. Latvian designer Tamara Orjola, for instance, is exploring applications for pine needles, a copious waste product as pine is the world's main source of timber. Employing only basic manufacturing processes such as crushing, soaking and steaming to lessen environmental impact, she has produced adaptable fibres that can be used for biodegradable papers, chairs and carpets, while creating essential oils and dyes as by-products.

Biofabrication

Some of the most eye-catching research within regenerative design is dedicated to the development of 'biological factories'. Through careful control of variables, biodegradable products can be grown with living organisms including algae, bacteria and fungi – the latter's threadlike mycelia, usually hidden underground, are especially promising in ease of cultivation and adaptability. Such organisms often consume waste, and supply both the materials and processes when manufacturing products, further 'closing the loop' and lessening consumption of finite resources.

Diverse bioplastics and fabrics are already being grown, the latter with patterns already in place, holding out the promise of customizable textiles with fittings incorporated. There are credible aspirations to develop the technologies for medicine, self-repairing buildings and even mycelium-based electronics, computers and communication networks. With significant investment and design ingenuity, the balance can be tipped away from existing manufacturing infrastructure, and the metamorphosis of the industrial base can begin.

Taking a closer look at underutilized plants and fibres can reveal their potential as a source of valuable eco-friendly materials. The robust wiry wool once destined for carpets has fallen out of favour, but is now being used by British company Solidwool to produce strong attractive composite materials that can be used for both panels and furniture. Similarly, Dutch designer Christien Meindertsma has created a chair out of woven and felted flax – a hardy plant growing across the world – adding in a bioplastic derived from corn starch, then heat-pressing a single sheet to make a totally biodegradable piece of furniture.

Meindertsma's Flax Chair is attractive, but also determinedly neutral, even beige, as are many similar projects using plants such as hemp and eelgrass for clothing, claddings and insulation. For these products to reach mass audiences and achieve their desired environmental impacts, it may be necessary for design, and its consumers, to put aside the abiding focus on perfection and durability inherited from early Modernism. Instead, the imperfect, patinated, tactile and even odiferous will need to be accepted, expressing its organic origins, and decaying naturally – and being seen to do so. But it will require a leap of imagination to accept that once-permanent products are now just one moment in a material's lifecycle.

The condensed idea
Regenerating resources, restoring nature

50 Craftivism

In January 2017, at the Women's March in Washington, DC, thousands of participants wore pink knitted hats with raised corners resembling ears, 'pussyhats', as a protest at the language and behaviour of the newly inaugurated president, Donald Trump. It was the moment when Craftivism – a term coined in 2003, crunching together 'craft' and 'activism', but with a hint of the more enigmatic 'crafty' – broke into mainstream consciousness. Since then, it has grown rapidly in profile and, occasionally, in controversy.

Deep roots

Too often, creative activities deemed suitable for women – usually domestic and related to textiles – have been labelled as craft. Implicitly or explicitly, they are categorized as decorative and superficial, lacking the 'genius' that would elevate them to the category of 'art'. Even when the resulting item has been created for sale, remuneration has often been negligible. However, whether categorized as craft, art or design – or perhaps all three – this 'women's work' can become a means to foster self-respect, community, resistance or even protest, turning an activity all too often associated with subjugation into one of empowerment. And this repurposing is a design activity in itself, involving a process of conception, production and execution.

Examples of woven protests can be found scattered throughout history, from abolitionist quilts made in the United States in the 1830s, to colourful patchwork *arpilleras* documenting human-rights abuses produced by unknown female artists in Chile in the 1970s, branded 'tapestries of defamation' by the authoritarian regime of Augusto Pinochet. Similarly moving are the handkerchiefs embroidered in enforced silence in London's Holloway Prison around 1910 – the height of the suffragette movement in Britain – featuring the names of women on hunger strike and often being force-fed, alongside such declarations as 'deeds not words' and 'votes for women'.

The coming of Craftivism

In tandem with wider appreciation of women's crafts from the 1960s onwards, Feminist artists like Faith Ringgold, with her narrative quilts,

The Pussyhat Project

While participating in knitting circles in late 2016, Jayna Zweiman and Krista Suh chatted about the Women's March planned for 21 January 2017 in Washington, DC, to protest at Donald Trump's misogyny, epitomized by leaked audio that included the phrase 'grab 'em by the pussy'. The result of these conversations was a simple downloadable pattern for a knitted 'pussyhat' that reclaimed Trump's term as one of empowerment. It also allowed those unable to attend to express solidarity by creating and sending hats to marchers, offering them a collective emblem and some respite from the weather. Complaints about the project have ranged across the choice of colour and name, as well as its symbolism and supposed triviality. Yet the visual impact, when news cameras panned over a sea of people wearing tens of thousands of pussyhats, was undeniable, making a moving collective statement. Within a month, a pussyhat was on the cover of *TIME* magazine. By the end of the year, they had entered the collections of the British Museum in London and the Smithsonian Institution in Washington, DC. Like the embroidered banners of velvet and silk carried by the suffragettes in the early 20th century, the pussyhat powerfully reconceived a 'feminine occupation' for political protest.

and Faith Wilding, with such installations as the womblike *Crocheted Environment* (1972), began to employ needlework, quilting and other techniques. In so doing, they reaffirmed the legitimacy of these skills as artistic undertakings, and the dignity of all who practised them in the past. Slowly, this goal became more explicit and more activist, shifting from artmaking to design practice, often resulting in projects that seem playful, but have serious social, political and environmental goals.

Finally given its name in 2003 by American writer and activist Betsy Greer, the Craftivism movement has manifested itself in many different countries. The UK-based Craftivist Collective employs 'gentle protest', with a focus on empathy, mindfulness and humility, for instance with its campaign in 2015 against low pay at leading department-store chain Marks & Spencer. The collective delivered hand-sewn handkerchiefs to board members, celebrities and investors at the chain's annual general meeting, each one carefully personalized to the individual's interests and concerns, as well as distributing 250 handkerchief kits to shareholders. The Mexican collective Bordamos Feminicidios is more assertive, embroidering first-person narratives of women murdered by their partners onto handkerchiefs to preserve their memory, then stitching them together to create striking banners to be carried at demonstrations. And there are occasional male Craftivist groups too, such as the Hombres Tejedores knitting collective in Chile, which questions dominant conceptions of masculinity and proposes gentler alternatives.

> **Craftivism is a way of looking at life where voicing opinions through creativity makes your voice stronger, your compassion deeper and your quest for justice more infinite.**
>
> Betsy Greer, 2007

Through Craftivism, those who struggle with the pressures of protest marches, civil disobedience and confrontation can engage in campaigning, often in mutually supportive groups. They can also make this participation visible in public spaces with activities such as guerrilla knitting. And, through this alternative approach, they can perhaps provide additional insights and traction to protests along the way. As such, Craftivism has been called 'activism for introverts', accessible to and involving all, not just the loudest. Allowing an increased range of people to engage in activism seems like a worthwhile undertaking. It also helps Craftivism arouse public interest in a way that critical design and other theory-focused movements can struggle to achieve.

There have been criticisms. Craftivism can feel like a middle-class, middle-of-the-road activity for those with time and resources, undertaken with insufficient urgency and impact to tackle very real, very immediate environmental and social problems. But the example of Bordamos Feminicidios suggests that Craftivism doesn't have to be reticent. In any case, as the founder of the Craftivist Collective, Sarah Corbett, puts it, 'Craft, if done wisely, can be a powerful, change-making instrument to add to the toolbox of activism.'

The condensed idea
Making design matter

Glossary

Biomorphism Design derived from, or evoking, natural organic forms or patterns.

CAD/CAM (Computer-aided design/ manufacture) The use of computers to create and improve designs, and to control machines for their manufacture.

Circular economy A model of production and consumption in which materials are kept in circulation through processes such as reuse, refurbishment and recycling.

Decorative arts Collective term for the vast class of objects intended as both functional and beautiful, including furniture, ceramics, glass, metalwork, textiles; distinguished from 'fine arts', principally painting and sculpture.

Division of labour The separation of tasks in manufacture and other activities for execution by a specific person or group, to maximize efficiency and economy.

Ergonomics The study of human physical interaction with technology and products, to ensure health and safety, and to optimize outputs.

Feedback loop A circuit of self-correcting action and reaction, positive or negative; often used to describe improvement following consumer experience and consultation.

Fordism Named after Henry Ford, whose Model T (1908) was the first mass-produced car. Fordism expresses industrialization at full tilt, with extensive production lines, wholesale systematization, higher wages and higher profits.

Formalism A design approach that prioritizes form (appearance and composition) above other factors, including functionality and practicality.

Functionalism A theory of design that emphasizes construction and purpose, and disdains ornament, drawing on the phrase 'form follows function' (Louis Sullivan, 1896).

Gesamtkunstwerk A composite and complete work of art that unifies a range of techniques, materials and concepts into more than the sum of its parts.

Gothic A style of architecture characterized by the pointed arch, first developed near Paris around 1140 and thence spread throughout Europe; revived in England from around 1750 and spread internationally.

Graphical user interface (GUI) An interface allowing users to interact with digital devices via graphical elements, for instance windows, buttons, cursors and icons, rather than text.

Historicism The application of historic styles to modern designs, sometimes stereotyped as a Victorian development, but a more-or-less perennial phenomenon.

Humanism From 1300–1600, a revival of classical learning permeated Western art, since which time the worth and potential of the human has served as a touchstone for design.

Interchangeability The industrial manufacture of parts that are for practical purposes identical, and thus reliably applicable to similar objects.

International Style The leading Modernist movement in architecture from the 1920s onwards, focusing on functionality, minimalism and universalism; also applied, as the International Typographic Style, to the associated graphic design style developed largely in Switzerland from the 1940s.

Just-in-time manufacturing Responding to specific orders through instant communications and faster, more flexible manufacture and transport, eliminating the need to hold stock, which ties up capital and space.

Lean production A manufacturing process that focuses on the systematic elimination of waste and redundancy in order to achieve economy and efficiency, drawing on the Toyota Production System developed in Japan from the 1950s.

Modularity In design and architecture, the reduction of projects into independent components capable of flexible combination and configuration.

Neoclassicism The revival of ancient Greek and Roman architecture and ornament from around 1750, often associated with purity and rationality.

Neoplasticism In the magazine *De Stijl* (1917), Piet Mondrian proposed a new theory of art, 'Nieuwe Beelding', espousing rigorous abstraction, using lines and colour to achieve spiritual validity and beauty.

New Objectivity A translation of the German *Neue Sachlichkeit*, a term coined in 1924 to describe a group of artists focused on the practical, functional and down-to-earth, rejecting ornament and expressionist indulgence.

Piecework A system by which workers are paid for individual products or tasks and not by time.

Rationalism Used from the 1920s onwards to indicate a design approach that focuses on geometrical purity, structural clarity and functional honesty, prioritizing objectivity and practicality above ornament.

Sans serif A typeface with the 'serifs' – the traditional small projections at the ends of characters – removed, generating a modern aesthetic popular from the 1920s onwards.

Semiotics The study of signs conveying meanings burgeoned after 1900, particularly in 1960s France, leading in design to an increasingly sophisticated manipulation of forms and images to communicate messages.

Standardization The design and manufacture of parts and products in standard forms to facilitate mass production and interchangeability. Also the development and application of agreed specifications across industries, sectors and nations to ensure compatibility and safety.

Streamlining From the 1930s, forms designed to minimize resistance, predominantly curvilinear and usually horizontal, and thus expressive of speed and modernity, have been applied to objects of every kind, however stationary.

Studio pottery The burgeoning of pottery created by individuals or small studios since 1900, influenced by China and Japan, with results ranging from the stolidly functional to the abstract and enigmatic.

Suprematism Conceived by Kazimir Malevich in 1913, Suprematism proposed a severely abstract form of art designed to convey feelings: his *Black Square* (1915) was a manifesto.

Symbolism First developed in France and Belgium from about 1860 in opposition to Realism, Symbolism's pursuit of the poetic, the sensual, the mystic and the ideal spread throughout Europe.

Taylorism The theory and practice encapsulated in Frederick Winslow Taylor's groundbreaking *The Principles of Scientific Management* (1911), which advocated rigorous scientific analysis of work and expert management.

Universality An ideal of designs as universally acceptable and applicable; more recently an ideal focused on accessibility and the reconciliation of contrasting or conflicting requirements.

World expos The 1851 London Crystal Palace Great Exhibition of the Works of Industry of All Nations inspired a continuing series of such international events, known as 'expos' after the French *exposition*.

Index

About the Author

John Jervis has served as deputy editor at *Icon* and managing editor for *ArtAsiaPacific*, writes on architecture and design for *Design Anthology*, *Apollo*, *RIBA Journal* and *Frame*, with a particular focus on (and love of) post-war megastructures, and works with Tate, Thames & Hudson and the National Gallery.

First published in Great Britain in 2024 by

Greenfinch
An imprint of Quercus Editions Limited
Carmelite House
50 Victoria Embankment
London EC4Y 0DZ

An Hachette UK company
The authorised representative in the EEA is Hachette Ireland, 8 Castlecourt Centre, Castleknock Road, Castleknock, Dublin 15, D15 YF6A, Ireland

A CIP catalogue record for this book is available from the British Library

PB ISBN 9781529439687
eBook ISBN 9781529439694

10 9 8 7 6 5 4 3 2 1

Typeset by Ginny Zeal

Printed and bound in Great Britain by Clays Ltd, Elcograf S.p.A

MIX
Paper | Supporting responsible forestry
FSC® C104740
www.fsc.org

Papers used by Greenfinch are from well-managed forests and other responsible sources.

Picture credits
Alamy: 25 JJs; 34 Pictorial Press Ltd; 38 WBC ART; 46 © Fine Art Images/Heritage Images; 62 Julian Castle/Arcaid Images; 65 Juergen Hanel; 78 Nick Harrison; 86 (left) cm studio; 86 (right) picsmart; 94 BFA; 121 YA/BOT; 134 fotodezign 10; 192 Charlie J Ercilla. **Getty Images:** 98 Apic. **Shutterstock:** 18 Universal History Archive/UIG; 126 Pixelsquid; 142 J.Mahaudomchab; 154 SEJWAL123; 182 Dennis M Sabangan/EPA; 201 eddie-hernandez.com.